Paradox is an authentic invitation to lean in and hear the sprawling ballad of freedom that rings out from the tension of seemingly contradictory truth. It is a loving dare to trust Jesus, whose very nature is a paradox, as he leads us on the adventure of faith, beyond our feeble attempts to rationalize or comprehend his love. Read it and let your spirit hum with the music of mercy.

—LEE ANDERSON, lead singer and songwriter of the band Look Homeward

In our broken world, it's easy to mistake our questions and struggles as deal-breakers to the gospel's foundational truths. *Paradox* encourages me to lean into these questions and struggles and creates a safe refuge to actively explore challenges I had previously passively sidestepped. I'd recommend this book to anyone looking to lean into hard questions. You'll find the light of the gospel shining from a fresh perspective.

—ABBY BOUCHON, education outreach specialist at Google

Eloquently written and full of truth, this book is a fount of knowledge and wisdom for people of all backgrounds, including those who do not consider themselves Christians. Rich, thoughtful, insightful, and provocative, LeRoy and Summers have written a gem that explains how things that are ostensibly paradoxical, such as belief and reason, are instead connected in a powerful way. I highly recommend it.

—CHRISTOPHER J. CLARK, assistant professor at UNC-Chapel Hill in the Department of Political Science and speaker for the Veritas Forum

It is one thing to have something to say and quite another to know how to say it. For many writers, it's a paradox—substance or style—and most have to choose. But LeRoy and Summers have both in this book, which is an overflow of their walks with God. Comparing things like grace and truth, they help us to see not only the importance of each but something more, like holiness, in the blending of them. *Paradox* is fresh in thought, deep in Scripture, and rooted in the holiness tradition. I thank God for these guys. They're part of the next generation of holiness writers.

—STEVE DENEFF, senior pastor of College Wesleyan Church, coauthor of *SoulShift* (WPH), and author of *FaultLines* (WPH)

This book tackles questions the everyday believer is too afraid to ask and pastors are too afraid to answer. If you're an intellectual struggling to make sense of the Bible's dichotomies, this is the book for you. It is written with a humility that normalizes doubt yet inspires the reader to press on in the pursuit of truth. *Paradox* is a must-read for all believers so they are exposed to difficult faith questions and inspired to continue asking questions and seeking answers about their belief in Jesus Christ.

—TAYLOR DIETMEIER, director of Uhuru Girls Secondary School in Kenya

In a culture that tries to avoid tension, this book does not. Scripture is full of tensions, yet Matt and Jeremy boldly take the tensions as faith enrichers. No avoidance here. No apologies. The brevity also makes for depth and every word a journey to embrace the tensions and discover the mystery of faith.

—JO ANNE LYON, general superintendent of The Wesleyan Church

The best leaders create simplicity in the midst of complexity. In *Paradox* Matt and Jeremy successfully lead us across the tightrope of tensions in our faith. We are gifted with this book in a time when Christians are often encouraged to reject tension and stay off the rope. Allow *Paradox* to reintroduce you to the wonder of the walk.

—HEATHER SEMPLE, lead pastor of Red Cedar Church

When it comes to the tensions we find in our faith, we want clear-cut answers. It's easier that way. It's safer. But this book is for the brave Christians and honest skeptics. For the ones who refuse to shut out or explain away the difficult questions and instead dare to wrestle with them.

—ADAM WEBER, founding pastor of Embrace Church and author of *Talking with God*

With artistry LeRoy and Summers creatively call us away from the tidy, domesticated either/or approach to Scripture and life. Instead, we are compelled to embrace the complexity and vibrancy of both/and that we might hear the call to enter the dance of God. I found myself contemplating and underlining numerous truths rich with wisdom that I look forward to passing on to others.

—JR WOODWARD, director of V3 Church Planting Movement and author of *The Church as a Movement* and *Creating a Missional Culture*

PARADOX

EMBRACING THE TENSIONS OF CHRISTIANITY

Matt LeRoy
Jeremy Summers

wesleyan
PUBLISHING HOUSE
wphstore.com

Copyright © 2016 by Matt LeRoy and Jeremy Summers
Published by Wesleyan Publishing House
Indianapolis, Indiana 46250
Printed in the United States of America
ISBN: 978-1-63257-091-8
ISBN (e-book): 978-1-63257-092-5

Library of Congress Cataloging-in-Publication Data

LeRoy, Matthew, author.
Paradox : embracing the tensions of Christianity / Matt LeRoy and
   Jeremy Summers.
Indianapolis : Wesleyan Publishing House, 2016.
LCCN 2015050105 | ISBN 9781632570918 (pbk.)
LCSH: Theology, Doctrinal--Popular works.
LCC BT77 .L346 2016 | DDC 230--dc23 LC record available at http://lccn.loc.gov/
2015050105

All Scripture quotations, unless otherwise indicated, are taken from the Holy
Bible, New International Version®, NIV ®. Copyright ©1973, 1978, 1984, 2011 by
Biblica, Inc. Used by permission. All rights reserved worldwide.

Cover design: Cody Rayn

Contents

For additional free resources, visit
wphresources.com/paradox.

Introduction

Many elements of our faith are in tension with each other. We often see them as opposites, diametrically opposed to one another, but they are not. Yes, tension exists between them, but not the kind of tension that pushes them apart. Instead, like the dynamic tension within an atom or a spring, this tension holds them together and makes them function.

Our friend Jason helped us see this using the strings on his guitar as an illustration. He reminded us that the tension in the strings is exactly what makes the sound possible. You could remove that tension, but you lose the song in the process.

The same is true with our understanding of God. Over the centuries, people have tried to remove the essential tensions within God's character by declaring, for example, that Jesus was either fully human or fully divine but not both; or that God is either all-powerful or all good but not both. But, as with the guitar strings, when we remove the tension from our understanding of God, we lose the beauty as well as the truth. Some aspects of God's character can only be understood in the tension between two seemingly opposite concepts. That's where the music comes from. Therefore it is crucial to learn the discipline of embracing tension, for this beautiful complexity creates the music and mystery of our faith.

1

Grace & Truth

Imagine for a moment that you are forced to stand in front of a roomful of people—at work, at school, at church, or at a family gathering—and you have no idea why. Are you receiving an award? A promotion? A public thank you? A leader whom you respect starts to speak, and the purpose of the gathering becomes clear. The leader begins to reveal, before a crowd of shocked onlookers, your deepest, darkest secret, the one thing you have labored to keep from seeing the light. You have managed to skillfully redirect any conversation away from it, but now it is laid out in the open for all to see. There is nowhere to hide, no way to recover. You are exposed.

In John 8, we meet a woman caught in a storm of shame and guilt. She was exposed. Her secret was revealed, and the revelation not only cost her dignity but also threatened her life.

At dawn he appeared again in the temple courts, where all the people gathered around him, and he sat down to teach them. The teachers of the law and the Pharisees brought in a woman caught in adultery. They made her stand before the group and said to Jesus, "Teacher, this woman was caught in the act of adultery. In the Law Moses commanded us to stone such women. Now what do you say?" They were using this question as a trap, in order to have a basis for accusing him. But Jesus bent down and started to write on the ground with his finger. When they kept on questioning him, he straightened up and said to them, "Let any one of you who is without sin be the first to throw a stone at her." Again he stooped down and wrote on the ground. At this, those who heard began to go away one at a time, the older ones first, until only Jesus was left, with the woman still standing there. Jesus straightened up and asked her, "Woman, where are they? Has no one condemned you?" "No one, sir," she said. "Then neither do I condemn you," Jesus declared. "Go now and leave your life of sin." (John 8:2–11)

The teachers of the law and the Pharisees tried to trap Jesus with an embarrassing dilemma. It is a familiar setup that we've seen many times before. On one occasion the religious experts came to Jesus and tested him with a tax question. They asked whether it was lawful for Jewish people to pay taxes to Caesar's Roman Empire. Seeing through their motives, Jesus easily evaded the trap by asking for a coin. "Whose face is this," he asked, "and whose inscription?" "Caesar's," they answered. "Then give back to Caesar what is Caesar's," Jesus said, "and to God what is God's" (see Luke 20:20–25). Caesar's image is stamped on the coin, so give it to him. But God's image is stamped on you, so give yourself fully to God.

At another time, the Pharisees came with a technical, theologically loaded question about the law: Which is the greatest commandment? Far from seeking Jesus' wisdom on the issue, they hoped to trap him in his own words. If he emphasized one commandment, they could accuse him of neglecting the others. Again we see Jesus' genius on display. His brilliant answer somehow tied together the entire sweep of Scripture: "Love the Lord your God with all you are and all you have. And love others in this same reckless and ridiculous way. All of the Law and the Prophets hang on these two ideas" (see Matt. 22:37–40).

But wait, is that cheating? They asked for one command, and Jesus gave them two. By doing so, Jesus showed that these commands are like two sides of a coin. You can't separate them or choose between the two. This is like breathing for a Christian. Which is more important, breathing in or breathing out? If you aren't doing both, you will soon do neither.

Now they came again, these same religious leaders, plotting to trap Jesus with a difficult question and thereby undercut his authority in the eyes of the people. Only this time they didn't use a coin or commandment as bait. They used a human life. Trading in the social currency of family and personal honor, so highly valued in ancient Middle Eastern culture, the religious experts paraded this woman in the public temple courts where there was no escape from her gut-wrenching guilt. She was exposed, her dark secret dragged into the light of day.

They dropped her at his feet, pitting his compassion for sinners against his love for justice. So which will it be, Jesus, grace or truth? Will you choose grace and continue to win the hearts of the people with your compelling vision of the kingdom of God? Or will you choose truth and stand with the time-honored tradition of Moses' law, the very sign of God's covenant with Israel? Grace or truth?

The trap was set.

MOSES AND JESUS

As the religious leaders drew the battle line between Moses and Jesus, it was clear which side they stood on. They were passionate about observing and protecting the sacred law of Moses. Until we take a closer look.

Did you notice that someone is missing from this story? Yes, the law of Moses instructs that this woman, guilty of adultery, should be stoned. But that is only half of the command because she was only one of the guilty parties. Which begs the question, where was the man? The woman was caught in the act of adultery, so her partner must have been also. Why didn't they drag him into the public square as well? At best, it appears that these teachers of the law were demanding that Jesus give an exact answer about the law while they carefully edited the facts of the case.

At worst, it could be that the man was part of the plot. We can't know, of course, but at the very least he seems to have been used to set up this entire scenario. In their animosity toward Jesus, did the Pharisees induce a man to seduce this woman? If that was the case, they had lured two people into sin in order to defame a third.

Either way, they were twisting the law in an attempt to prove that Jesus didn't respect the law. The most revered religious leaders of the community were willing to steal the dignity and trade the life of a daughter of Israel in order to deal a blow to Jesus' reputation. The hypocrisy of this moment is breathtaking.

Notice, too, that this trap not only pitted Jesus against Moses but also maneuvered him into a stance against Rome. Israel was no longer a sovereign kingdom. They lived under the Roman Empire's oppressive rule; Rome had removed their right to conduct executions. Rome was more than happy to execute lawbreakers, and they had honed this skill to perfection—which is why Jesus was crucified according to Roman law, not stoned as Jewish law dictates. In order to put him to death for blasphemy against Yahweh, the religious establishment argued that his claim to be king was a threat to Rome.

So back to our story, if Jesus allowed this woman to be stoned, he risked the retribution of the Roman governor against his people. Many lives were at stake in this test case. Jesus was cornered, trapped between grace or truth, hemmed in by Moses and Rome. What would he do?

Without a word, he bent down and wrote in the dirt with his finger. Sensing they had him on the defensive, the religious leaders pressed the attack, demanding an answer to decide the fate of the woman. But Jesus, still silent, continued to write.

What was he writing? No one knew, and it doesn't matter. As the ancient fathers of the church pointed out, the meaning is not in the words written but in the one writing. The teachers of the law questioned his commitment to the law, but they didn't realize that he was the one who wrote the law. The finger that drew in the dust was the very finger that etched the law into stone in blaze and glory. And we shudder to realize that it's entirely possible to accumulate a lifetime of nuanced knowledge about the Word yet fail to know the Word himself.

IF ANY ONE OF YOU IS WITHOUT SIN

Finally, Jesus stood up and gave an answer. "Let any one of you who is without sin be the first to throw a stone at her" (John 8:7).

Don't rush past that. Breathe it in. Don't allow yourself to become so familiar with these famous words that the wonder of them escapes you.

In this brilliant moment, Jesus spoke both grace and truth. He upheld the law of Moses and extended the Father's heart of compassion. He didn't take a watered-down middle way. He didn't straddle the line to avoid controversy. Instead, Jesus lifted his vision above the false dichotomy of compassion and justice and saw the full picture in a way that no one else can, not without his revelation. He embraced the tension, and held seeming opposites in perfect harmony.

Jesus bent down and began writing in the sand again. In the silence, clarity sets in. Now we see that this story is about not only the power of grace but also the ugliness of sin. The religious leaders—their sins were exposed as well, their hearts as hard as the stones in their hands. With quiet yet irresistibly powerful insight, Jesus revealed that everyone present was plagued by sin, and he alone was immune.

Beginning with the oldest, and presumably the wisest, the accusers walked away one by one. The woman heard the sound of stones hitting the ground. One damning accusation after another falling flat, empty of the power to condemn. The sound of those stones hitting the ground were like drumbeats in the anthem of grace.

This is the strength of grace: not that Jesus overlooks sin but that he looks it in the eye, calls it what it is, and overthrows it. Jesus does not condone sin. He risks something far more courageous. He forgives it. He alone had the power to condemn this woman. He alone had the right to cast a stone. And Jesus does judge sin. He took the judgment upon himself on the cross, where mercy and justice, grace and truth collide. And so he declared his judgment to this woman: "Neither do I condemn you" (John 8:11).

He makes the same declaration to you and me.

GO NOW AND LEAVE YOUR LIFE OF SIN

The same grace that extends forgiveness empowers freedom. Grace produces holiness of heart and life. Grace initiates salvation and continues its work by enabling obedience and surrender and transformation.

Jesus doesn't just send a message of pardon into our dungeons of guilt. He fights his way to us, throws open the prison doors, and breaks every chain that holds us captive. With the battle wounds still fresh on his hands and head, he leads us into the life of freedom he has won for us.

People often say that there is a time for showing grace and a time for speaking truth, as if it were possible to dissect and disconnect the attributes of the Sovereign God. We are quick to fragment God's character, while in Jesus we find it held firmly together. We do not choose between grace and truth, and we do not need to. John said Jesus came to us full of grace and truth. He embodies both. The tension between these two virtues doesn't pull them apart; it binds them together.

Grace is truth. And truth is grace.

Grace is truth because there is nothing truer in this world than God's extravagant love and our desperate need for it. And truth is grace because it is a gift from God, showing our desperate need for him and the way to be reconciled.

As we awaken to truth, we gain a decidedly optimistic view of what grace can accomplish. Jesus does more than forgive our past; he redeems our present and reclaims our future. He changes the trajectory of our lives and commands we live in response to that redemption. Our lives become evidence of the power of grace. "Neither do I condemn you" comes before and paves the way for "go and leave your life of sin." It is never the other way around.

Many of us hold on to rocks, not that we aim at others, but that are evidence of our own guilt. We refuse to let go of the shame we have been dragging around for years. Jesus gives us the freedom to drop the stones. Let go and experience the transformative power of both grace and truth, embodied in our Savior, Jesus.

2

CHURCH & CULTURE

"Human beings will be happier," Kurt Vonnegut said, "not when they cure cancer or get to Mars . . . but when they find ways to inhabit primitive communities."[1] Vonnegut was a controversial author and isn't often quoted in support of Christianity. Yet his poignant observation perfectly captures our primal hunger for authentic expressions of the church.

Two centuries earlier another firebrand and provocateur named John Wesley called for a rediscovery of what he named "the primitive church." Referring to the early church as described in the New Testament, Wesley believed the dynamic spiritual and social renaissance those early believers experienced could happen again in his day. For having the audacity to vocalize such faith in the unchanging nature of God, the once-prestigious Mr. Wesley was rewarded by being banned from church pulpits in London. At the encouragement of a close friend, Wesley took to preaching outdoors to the poor and forgotten. He even resorted to proclaiming his message from atop his father's tombstone, reasoning that no one could ban him from that one spot. Still he was resisted both verbally and physically by people who thought he desecrated the Holy Word by carrying it to the margins of society.

A strange thing happened as Wesley went from promising young Oxford fellow to outcast itinerant preacher. When he was forced beyond the walls of the established, institutionalized church, the gospel took root in the culture around him. It was as if the wild thicket of culture was the kingdom's native habitat. As increasing numbers of people experienced the hope of Jesus, Wesley strategically organized them into small, nimble groups for growth and accountability. These environments also produced multiplication. As disciples made more disciples, these micro-movements worked their way through England with exponential speed. The poor and marginalized both received and served. Ordinary people were empowered to expand the kingdom. Unlikely voices discovered the gift of preaching, and other improbable souls found the ability to lead and shepherd. The Holy Spirit indeed revived a vision of the primitive church, proving that the time ripest for renewal is always now. Historians theorize that the Wesleyan revival had such a transformative impact on the culture that it drew England back from the brink of a violent revolution.

Historian Donald Dayton pointed out that the church, at its best, can't be described as either liberal or conservative.[2] Those labels are too weak and miss the point. A better designation is "radical." We often think that the word *radical* implies extremism.

It actually comes from the Latin term *radix*, which means "root." The radical church returns to its roots and finds a way to inhabit primitive communities again. By remembering our story, we rediscover our DNA and live into inherited family traits. Our genetic map points the way forward. Our memory sets our imagination on fire. As A. W. Tozer said, "Whatever new thing anyone discovers is already old, for it is the present expression of a previous thought of God."[3] Perhaps we don't need to create new ways of doing church. The ancient past can reveal God's vision for the future—an authentic expression of the church, a church neither fleeing from nor fighting against culture but transforming it from within.

ECCLESIA DNA

The New Testament word that we often translate as "church" is *ecclesia*. This powerful little word holds the potential to help us rediscover our calling and design. Locked inside this Greek term is the DNA of the church—what it was and what it can be in the world again.

For starters, *ecclesia* doesn't exactly mean church, as we usually think of it. After the church was launched with power on the day of Pentecost, the first believers didn't create a new term to describe who they were. They borrowed an existing term, already invested with meaning. *Ecclesia* means "assembly, gathering, or congregation." The word refers to a body of people, not to a building. Interestingly, our English word *church* is derived from the German word *kirche*, which generally *does* refer to the church building. Do you see the difference between these concepts? One is a place, and the other is people. One is brick and mortar, and the other is flesh and blood.

This dynamic little term, *ecclesia*, holds another layer of meaning. Digging deeper, we find that it is a compound of two words meaning "to summon" and "out." So its root meaning is "called-out ones." And in this we find the DNA of the church—we are the called-out ones.

What does that mean for us? How does that reorient us to our purpose? To find out, let's look at each of those three defining words.

CALLED

How did this entire movement, the church, begin? Jesus called disciples. And that call continues with us. We are called by Jesus to follow him wherever he leads, whatever that costs. This is the DNA strand called *discipleship*.

"Come, follow me" is a simple invitation. But hidden in those words is the power to reroute the trajectory of our lives. When the first disciples, who were fishermen, heard the call, they immediately dropped their nets and stepped into the future, ultimately reshaping the world. Across the generations, Jesus' invitation has not changed, yet it continues to change everything. Modern-day disciples answer the same call to follow Jesus into the new life that he pioneers, leaving a trail of transformation in his wake.

But let's be real about this: The stakes are high, and the cost is steep. Jesus offers no map, framework, or turn-by-turn description of where this journey will take us. He offers only the challenge to follow wherever he chooses to lead. There is no sales pitch about an easier life, no guarantee of greatness. There is just a call to surrender, with a warning that this choice will cost you everything.

So the call goes out and the cost is clear, but the question remains: Are you in? Will you trust Jesus and risk it all? Will you follow him into a life of discipleship?

OUT

This simple word sets our direction. We are called out. But where exactly is out? That depends on where God is. If God is located in a single, sacred space that we visit on one sacred day each week, then we are called to where he is—out of the world and into a building. In that case, the church would be an escape from culture and effectively serve itself in the name of personal holiness and fidelity. But if God is in the world, at work in every corner of creation, alive in every need, and bringing redemption to the broken places of our own communities and beyond, then we are called to where he is—out of the building and into the world, joining him in his mission to reconcile all things and all people to himself. This represents the DNA strand of mission.

After the victory of his crucifixion and resurrection, Jesus appeared to his disciples and commissioned them. As he prepared to ascend in glory to take his place at the Father's right hand, he cast the vision for the disciples' future by giving a clear command: Go and make more disciples. He sent them out on mission. Sending is intrinsic to Christianity because it fits a pattern in the character of God.

God sent Moses.

God sent prophets.

God sent John the Baptist.

God sent his Son.

Jesus sent the disciples.

God sent the Holy Spirit.

The Holy Spirit sends the church.

Mission is encoded in our DNA because we inherited it from our Father.

ONES

This last word reminds us that *ecclesia* is a collective noun. Our faith is shared. We are on a journey together. We see the Acts of the apostles marked by passionate worship of God, shocking compassion toward strangers, and the awe-inspiring power of the Holy Spirit. The first Christians were also known for the way they loved one another. Authentic community was a pillar of their existence, giving the church an irresistible beauty. "All the believers were together and had everything in common. They sold property and possessions to give to anyone who had need" (Acts 2:44–45). This description (and prescription) of the early church captures the imagination of their culture and has intrigued dreamers in every generation since.

Fellow dreamer Joe Sircar observed, "History is littered with attempts to create utopian societies. Governments, nonprofits, churches. But all of those dreams fail when we don't surrender our community to the Holy Spirit."[4]

There it is. The mystery of this early Christian community is discovered in its all-out surrender to the Holy Spirit. They were not communists. Communism is a failed form of human government, and every form of human government falls short of this ideal. Neither were they a capitalist democracy. Rather, in their submission to God and each other, they were a community empowered and governed by the Holy Spirit, a stunning answer to Jesus' prayer that they would be one.

The DNA of the church is discipleship (called), mission (out), and community (ones). In discipleship the love of Jesus and the power of the Holy Spirit lead us into the heart of the Father. In mission the heart of the Father sends us out in the power of the Spirit and the love of Jesus. And both must happen in community. Churches do not need separate programs for discipleship and mission. Both impulses should be intertwined in a double helix, bound by beads of community.

THE NEW PROTAGONISTS

The apostle Paul is known for using military imagery to represent our faith. In Ephesians 6:10–17, he pictured the believer wearing the armor of God, and encouraged us to be strong in the mighty power of God and stand against evil. Yet he clarified that "our struggle is not against flesh and blood" (Eph. 6:12). And when he spoke of our relationship with others, he clearly and decisively moved from military images to diplomatic language.

In 2 Corinthians 5:20, Paul wrote, "We are therefore Christ's ambassadors, as though God were making his appeal through us." As though God were making his appeal through us! We are a delegation representing the Sovereign God on a diplomatic mission in the world. Our task is to present the compelling love of Jesus to those around us. We are a mobile embassy of the kingdom of God. We are a safe house, a refuge, an oasis of heaven, a home for exiles in a foreign land.

Too often the church is combative, as if we were the antagonist in the story of church versus culture. We are seen as caring more about political issues than about people. However, our true agenda is to advance not the talking points of any political party but the culture of God's kingdom. Every day Jesus, in and through you, continues to stand in the face of Pilate to declare the revolutionary ethic of the kingdom of God. We are not the antagonists in the story; we are the protagonists. And we must be known more for who we are for than for what we are against. We must be known for how we love not for what we hate, not for critiquing culture from the outside but for transforming it from the inside.

THE LIGHT OF THE WORLD

In delivering his revolutionary Sermon on the Mount, Jesus sat on a hillside, opened his mouth, and changed the world. In that brilliant message, he conveyed a stunning vision of the kingdom come, revealing both who God is and who we are to be in response to him.

"You are the light of the world," Jesus said (Matt. 5:14). What a disruptive thought. We know and understand that Jesus is the Light of the World. But with that statement, he turned our previous notion on its head, drawing us into the story by declaring that we share his role as light-bringer to the darkened creation. Once we have encountered the light, we become carriers of the light. As one poet wrote, "[We] are the lanterns, and you are the light."[5] God fills us with his radiance and holds us out to a dark world as beacons of hope and grace.

Jesus continued, "You are the light of the world. A town built on a hill cannot be hidden. Neither do people light a lamp and put it under a bowl. Instead they put it on its stand, and it gives light to everyone in the house. In the same way, let your light shine before others, that they may see your good deeds and glorify your Father in heaven" (Matt. 5:14–16).

Darkness breeds despair. We empathize with the person whose faith has faded under the weight of darkness. It is understandable that someone might see tragedy, pain, suffering, and evil and begin to doubt that God exists. If there is a good and loving God, why is there so much heartbreak in the world? But pain and suffering do not disprove the existence of God; they prove the existence of humans. And if darkness breeds despair, what will light generate? Even the slightest flicker sends darkness on the run. Jesus said that our good works of great love will point people to our Father in heaven. As lanterns filled with the light, we are the counterargument to despair, illuminating the source of hope. Our lives should be the most compelling evidence. Perhaps one day others will begin to ask, "If there is not a good and loving God, then how in the world do you explain these people?" Albert Day was a pastor in the 1960s from that "exotic" land known as Ohio. He once said, "True holiness is a witness that cannot be ignored. Real sainthood is a phenomenon to which even the [skeptic] pays tribute. The power of a life, where Christ is exalted, would arrest and subdue those who are bored to tears by our thin version of Christianity."[6] Let us be the light, illuminating a countercultural, compelling, alternate vision of what can be.

SHINE LIKE STARS

In Philippians 2:15, Paul drew on this same imagery, challenging us to "shine . . . like stars." There is much freedom and grace in these words. As the Holy Spirit inspired his writing, Paul didn't reach for more dramatic or explosive imagery. He didn't tell us to burn like wildfire, shake the ground like an earthquake, or turn our city upside down like a whirlwind. He said to shine like stars. He did not ask for moments of greatness but his words push us to be a simple, humble, and consistent light in the deepest darkness.

George MacDonald was a Scottish pastor, poet, and author whose influence outpaces his fame. Though his name is not as widely recognized, he was a friend and mentor to Lewis Carroll. After reading the manuscript of Carroll's *Alice in Wonderland* to his children, MacDonald encouraged Carroll to publish the work for the world to enjoy. MacDonald was a key inspiration for later writers as well, including favorites such as J. R. R. Tolkien, C. S. Lewis, G. K. Chesterton, and Madeleine L'Engle. Reportedly, MacDonald's literary contemporary Mark Twain couldn't stand him—until he met him. MacDonald's humble countenance and substantive intellect won over Twain.[7]

In one of his poems for children, "A Baby Sermon," MacDonald beautifully captured the spirit of Paul's challenge:

> The lightning and thunder
> They go and they come;
> But the stars and the stillness
> Are always at home.[8]

We are not asking you to be a bolt of lightning. The world already has enough flash. We are not asking you to boom like thunder. There's more than enough noise. We are asking you to shine like stars—consistent, present light when the darkness is the deepest.

This kind of life will capture the imagination of the culture around us. As we rediscover and live into our embedded DNA as the *ecclesia*, we will remember our origins. We are the called-out ones. As one, we will follow Jesus into the broken places of our world and join him where he has long been at work. The time ripest for renewal is always now. A spiritual and social renaissance awaits. May we find ways to inhabit primitive communities again for the future of the church, for the glory of God, for the reach of the gospel, and for the sake of the world.

NOTES

1. Kurt Vonnegut, *Conversations with Kurt Vonnegut*, ed. William Rodney Allen (Jackson: University Press of Mississippi, 1988), 80.

2. Donald Dayton, "Prequel Lex: Reengaging Wesleyan Distinctives in God's Mission" (lecture, The Wesleyan Church General Conference, Lexington, KY, June 2, 2012).

3. A. W. Tozer, *Evenings with Tozer: Daily Devotional Readings*, comp. Gerald B. Smith (Chicago: Moody, 1981), February 16 entry.

4. Joseph Sircar, "Radical Community" (sermon, Love Chapel Hill Church, Chapel Hill, NC, August 31, 2014).

5. Arcade Fire, "Antichrist Television Blues," recorded 2007, on *Neon Bible*, Merge Records, accessed April 11, 2016, http://www.metrolyrics.com/antichrist-television-blues-lyrics-arcade-fire.html.

6. Albert Day, quoted in Reuben P. Job and Norman Shawchuck, eds., *A Guide to Prayer* (Nashville: Upper Room, 1983), 91.

7. "George MacDonald," *Wikipedia*, last updated February 9, 2016, https://en.wikipedia.org/wiki/George_MacDonald.

8. George MacDonald, *The Poetical Works of George MacDonald*, vol. 2 (London: Chatto & Windus, Picadilly, 1893), 160.

3

WORK & WORSHIP

Where do you spend most of your time during the week? What activities or efforts demand the majority of your energy and attention? For most of us, the answer would be work. Work consumes a massive portion of our lives, yet we rarely talk about how it is connected to our relationship with God. If Jesus is King of our lives, then his reign must reach into every realm of it, including our work.

At times we can miss the connection between work and worship. We work all week in the "real" world, then we retreat to worship in a sacred space on one sacred day. Rarely do we envision an overlap between the two. We see worship as a chance to get filled up for the week ahead, then we try to push through the work week until we get back to worship again. This is a small view of both activities that keeps them separated. So how do we expand our vision of the two? The answer is found not by taking more time away from our jobs to spend in church. The answer is to begin seeing our work as worship.

It is critical to understand and view work through this theological, biblical, Christ-centered, and gospel-driven lens because work has such potential to shape who we are. Obviously, work demands much of our time and energy. And it can also claim our identities. It has this power because we often connect who we are to what we do for a living. When you meet someone for the first time, a common introductory question is "What do you do?" And how do we answer? We say our job titles.

I am a teacher.

I am a doctor.

I am an artist.

I am an entrepreneur.

I am a farmer.

I am a police officer.

But notice that we don't say what we actually do in those jobs.

I teach.

I practice medicine.

I create.

I lead a startup.

I plant and harvest.

I serve and protect.

Why? Because we culturally and naturally associate what we do with who we are. Another way to see this is to remember childhood dreams. How did you express your hopes for the future? You didn't talk only about what you wanted to do. Most likely, you spoke about who you wanted to be. Work influences identity. Therefore, it is crucial to submit our work to the lordship of Jesus. It is imperative we understand that work and worship are intimately intertwined. It's time to sanctify the 9 to 5. If we don't, we will not keep our identities intact.

IN THE BEGINNING

As we look at Scripture, we see that work has been an important part of God's design for humanity from the beginning. In Genesis 2:15, our origin story tells us that God placed Adam in the garden to care for and cultivate Eden. That was before sin entered the picture in chapter 3, so according to Genesis, work is a part of God's original design for human beings. It is even portrayed as a part of paradise. Work is not just something we are forced to do, but something we are made to do. We can find rich joy, purpose, and meaning in it.

What kind of work were you made for?

What were you designed to do?

As we look closer at the story, we see exactly what kind of work humanity was intended for. God is the one who creates, sustains, and makes the garden grow. So why did God tell Adam to cultivate the garden? Because from the beginning, God has invited us to partner with him in making his creation flourish, not because he needs us but because he wants us to join him where he already is at work in the world. The aim of our work is to glorify God by making his creation flourish.

Proverbs 18:9 casts a tragic vision of what happens when we fail at this task. The wisdom writer said, "One who is slack in his work is brother to one who destroys." Faithful work cultivates flourishing, but to do poor work is to partner in the destruction of the world. Poor work sets the slow process of decay in motion. Eventually, the effects are felt by the character within and the culture beyond.

What does this mean in the context of your job? What does it look like? If you are a journalist, it means that you tell good stories and give yourself to spreading the truth. You don't take cheap shots, rejoice in the takedown, or feed the public appetite for mindless and vicious rumor. You don't thrive on division but engage in thoughtful speech. You help lower the polarizing volume while raising the level of productive discourse.

If you are a business owner, you think about your employees' quality of life, not just your own retirement plan. If you are the CEO of a corporation, you do what is right, not just what is technically legal. If you are a politician, you put doing what is best for the people before scoring points for a party. If you are a filmmaker, you inspire and challenge and provoke thought. You don't just appeal to the lowest common denominator of our broken culture. You spark reflection and imagination and hope. You join in with the flourishing. Work is worship. We offer it for the glory of God and for the sake of the world.

LEADING YOURSELF

This hopeful view of work may seem unrealistic based on the negative environment of your workplace. It's hard to cultivate the flourishing of creation in a dysfunctional setting. Maybe your boss is terrible or your manager doesn't inspire or lead you well.

So what?

As a result of the fall, we all have difficulties in our work. It's time for us to grow up and lead ourselves. If you can't lead yourself, you will never be trusted to lead others. Don't be the person who easily slips into the negative or cynical rhythm of your work environment. That is the easiest road to take, the common role to play. Write an alternative story in your place of work. Roll up your sleeves in that environment and get down to the good work of cultivating. Answer cynicism with creativity. Recognize that every moment you are on the clock is an opportunity to cast the compelling vision of how Jesus has transformed every single corner of your life. Your work is worship. It is a gift and an offering to God.

WORK IS MISSION

Work is also an opportunity to live out God's mission in the world. Jesus doesn't just invite us to believe; he calls us to follow. Then he commissions us to go. Every believer is a disciple, and every disciple is a missionary. "But I don't feel called to be a missionary." OK, fine. Are you a Christian? Your conversion is your call-

In this chapter, we explore how hope and suffering collide in his story by reading large portions of it, straight from Scripture. We let the author speak for himself, as he does so magnificently at the end of the book. This is a narrative that you may think you know well, but this ancient revelation deserves a fresh look.

Here is how the story begins: "In the land of Uz there lived a man whose name was Job. This man was blameless and upright; he feared God and shunned evil. . . . He was the greatest man among all the people of the East" (Job 1:1, 3).

From the outset, we see that Job was a man of God, walking in obedience and dynamic faith. He was highly revered, not only for his wealth and blessings but also for his relationship with God. And he was always mindful of that relationship. After his children would throw a celebration feast, it was Job's custom to offer a sacrifice to God on their behalf, thinking, "Perhaps my children have sinned and cursed God in their hearts" (Job 1:5). This shows how dedicated Job was to walking in right relationship with God. In fact, God had such confidence in the authenticity of Job's faith that he held him up as a standard of belief before a most unlikely character.

One day the angels came to present themselves before the LORD, and Satan also came with them. The LORD said to Satan, "Where have you come from?" Satan answered the LORD, "From roaming throughout the earth, going back and forth on it." Then the LORD said to Satan, "Have you considered my servant Job? There is no one on earth like him; he is blameless and upright, a man who fears God and shuns evil." "Does Job fear God for nothing?" Satan replied. "Have you not put a hedge around him and his household and everything he has? You have blessed the work of his hands, so that his flocks and herds are spread throughout the land. But now stretch out your hand and strike everything he has, and he will surely curse you to your face." The LORD said to Satan, "Very well, then, everything he has is in your power, but on the man himself do not lay a finger." Then Satan went out from the presence of the LORD. (Job 1:6–12)

You read that right. Satan entered God's presence, and God challenged him to take note of the pure and blameless faith of Job. God was convinced that no calamity from the Enemy could sway Job's trust. As the story continues, Satan put that theory to the test. He heaped death and destruction on Job's family and all he owned. Job lost everything at the hand of the Evil One. Only he and his wife survived.

There is an old maxim—an actual misquotation of 1 Corinthians 10:13—that says, "God will never give you more than you can handle." It's a nice thought, but it's not true. However, God will never give you more than *he* can handle for you. Job could not handle the pain and suffering inflicted on him by the Enemy. He was crushed, broken beyond belief. He wept and mourned. He tore his clothes and covered his head in ashes, a sign of utter despair. He could not understand why this had happened to him, yet in his confusion he worshiped God.

Job's three friends rushed to his side, sat with him, and mourned for seven days and seven nights. Once the period of mourning was over, they broke their silence. Gathering their collective wisdom and understanding, they opened their mouths and advised Job to repent. They pushed him to search his soul and discover what gruesome sin he must have harbored, what crime he must have committed against God that would merit such punishment. This was clearly an act of divine retribution, they said. Surely you have angered God. Why else would this judgment crash down upon your head? Find out what you did wrong, and make it right.

Meanwhile, Job's wife urged him to despair. "What kind of God would bring this on you when you have served him?" she wondered. "Curse him and die." But Job refused. Though he cursed his own life and the day he was born, he would not speak against God.

Then another character entered the story. His name was Elihu, and after Job's other three friends had had their say, Elihu spoke up. He said that, because he was a young man, he had held his tongue out of respect for his elders. But in his mind the time had come to inject his much-needed wisdom into the conversation. He began his speech this way: "But now, Job, listen to my words; pay attention to everything I say. I am about to open my mouth; my words are on the tip of my tongue" (Job 33:1–2). Elihu then made up for the time he had lost while waiting patiently, launching into an extended rant on Job's circumstances. For all of his hubris, Elihu's argument makes perfect sense. It is eloquent and persuasive. It is logical and convincing. As you read, you start to accept his conclusion that Job must have sinned and ushered all this calamity into his life.

This time Job did not answer the accusation. He did not speak up for himself because another voice suddenly broke in. Yahweh spoke.

> Then the Lord spoke to Job out of the storm. He said: "Who is this that obscures my plans with words without knowledge? Brace yourself like a man; I will question you, and you shall answer me. Where were you when I laid the earth's foundation? Tell me, if you understand. Who marked off its dimensions? Surely you know! Who stretched a measuring line across it? On what were its footings set, or who laid its cornerstone—while the morning stars sang together and all the angels shouted for joy? Who shut up the sea behind doors when it burst forth from the womb, when I made the clouds its garment and wrapped it in thick darkness, when I fixed limits for it and set its doors and bars in place, when I said, 'This far you may come and no farther; here is where your proud waves halt'? Have you ever given orders to the morning, or shown the dawn its place, that it might take the earth by the edges and shake the wicked out of it? . . ."

> The Lord said to Job: "Will the one who contends with the Almighty correct him? Let him who accuses God answer him!" Then Job answered the Lord: "I am unworthy—how can I reply to you? I put my hand over my mouth. I spoke

once, but I have no answer—twice, but I will say no more."
Then the LORD spoke to Job out of the storm: "Brace yourself
like a man; I will question you, and you shall answer me.
Would you discredit my justice? Would you condemn me
to justify yourself?" (Job 38:1–13; 40:1–8)

In the epilogue of the book, the narrator said God spoke to
Job's friends and commanded them to make a sacrifice for the way
they sinned against him by questioning Job's faith. After they did
that, God said, "My servant Job will pray for you, and I will accept
his prayer and not deal with you according to your folly. You have
not spoken the truth about me, as my servant Job has" (Job 42:8).
God restored not only Job's reputation in the sight of his friends
but also his joy, bringing healing to his soul on the other side of
tragic loss.

CORE TRUTHS

It is easy to see why Job's story captures our imagination, but
how are we to apply it to our lives? When we are faced with suffering, what can we learn from Job's experience? Here are four core
truths to take away from this narrative.

SUFFERING IS UNIVERSAL

Setting is an important part of any story. It is like another character. It doesn't have dialogue, but it always has something to say.

The setting of this story is Uz, a foreign land to the original audience of this story. Many of the characters have foreign names, and for the most part they refer to God by the generic name Elohim rather than the name he revealed to Moses, Yahweh. The narrator, on the other hand, called God Yahweh, suggesting that the narrator was of Jewish origin. Why does this matter? Because it reminds us that suffering is universal. And the cosmic question of how to find purpose in pain and loss is shared by humans across the barriers of time and space. Are you suffering? You are not in this alone.

KARMA IS A LIE

Not all suffering is cleanly and easily connected to sin. Suffering is not necessarily the result of God's judgment. Did Job's sin trigger this crushing wave of pain? Did God punish Job because he lacked sufficient faith? Did Job's trial persist because he failed to demonstrate the right kind of belief? By all means no. Karma, the idea that good fortune is a reward for good deeds and bad fortune is a punishment for evildoing, is a false theology and has no place in our faith. Don't beat up your friends with that misguided advice when what they really need is someone to sit in silence and mourn beside them.

The story of Job clearly tells us that what happened to Job wasn't because he didn't trust God but because God trusted Job. God knew that Job would not falter, even as the Enemy assailed him. The evil that befell Job was a direct attack from the Enemy. Don't blame God for what Satan does. Suffering is not a condemnation of our faith or a condemnation of God's character.

WE DON'T ALWAYS HAVE ANSWERS

As the book of Job comes to a close, we see that God never revealed the reason he allowed these tragedies to enter Job's life. The reader sees it, but Job did not. The same is true for us. We will not always see the full picture. We will not always get answers to our questions. Job did not receive answers, but he did experience the priceless gift of God's presence. This, of course, is the great twist in the human story. Throughout Scripture we see that God is *for* us, and this brings great courage and comfort. But perhaps the more profound discovery is that God is *with* us. The dominant symbol of Christianity around the world is the cross, the place where God suffered. The ultimate Innocent bore the weight of pain and suffering. From Job to Jesus, God enters into our pain and walks beside us. Practice that with your friends. Perhaps they don't need you to offer answers, but presence.

GOD REDEEMS SUFFERING

Even things done with evil intent can be brought into submission and redeemed for God's purpose and glory. God did not cause Job's suffering, but he did redeem it. God is sovereign, but that doesn't mean he causes evil. It means he is in control, even in the midst of the Evil One's most violent attacks. God is never surprised by what comes into your life and has the strength to hold you through it. He is not overthrown by evil or suffering; he has already defeated sin and death and hell, and he will overcome their threats against you. So the question is not "Why is God doing this to me?" but "How will God redeem this for my growth and his glory?"

THE UNION OF HOPE AND SUFFERING

You don't find hope in suffering. Hope finds you. Because God is already there, in the thick of it with you. Instead of asking how a good and loving God can allow suffering, perhaps we should ask, "What kind of God would enter into the suffering of his servants?" Suffering is not an argument against the goodness of God; it is a context for experiencing the love of God. And in this, we see that hope and suffering are not opposites. They are tangled together, as hope wades into our suffering and refuses to let us go.

5

REPENTANCE & REVIVAL

When we think of the prophet Jonah, we often think of a children's story. We associate it with memories of Sunday school and tales about a man and his friendly whale. Jonah is not a children's story. It is a gospel story, pointing us forward to the coming of Jesus, who was buried in the depths for three days and raised to life. And it is our story. We are Jonah. We come from a long line of people on the run from God. Often when we sense God leading in a clear direction, we hesitate at best or, far worse, plot a course in the opposite direction. And we wonder why we live in frustration.

The story of Jonah reminds us that repentance and revival are intimately connected. The former is not possible without the latter. As we confront the sin of the world, we must be honest about the sin within ourselves. Our repentance leads to revival, both in us and in the church, which in turn leads to repentance in the world—and the transformation of all.

NINEVEH NEEDED TO REPENT

In Jonah's story, God gave his prophet a mission: preach against the wicked city of Nineveh. Because of their evil and treacherous acts against others and their own twisted hearts, God commissioned Jonah to deliver a message of wrath and destruction to the Ninevites. In response, Jonah ran.

It is clear from the story that Jonah ran because he was afraid. But what, exactly, was he afraid of? One obvious answer is that Nineveh was a very powerful city in Jonah's time, so he was afraid of the retribution of the people. This city had a dreadful reputation for military conquest and brutality that would frighten anyone. But this was not the source of Jonah's fear.

Another option is that because the people were so entrenched in wickedness and their hearts hardened against God, Jonah knew they would ignore his message. It would be a hopeless mission with certain failure because of their hostility to the truth. No one wants to set out on an endeavor that has no chance of success. That would discourage any prophet, but it was not the source of Jonah's fear.

Then what was? The full answer is not revealed until the last chapter of the book. Jonah 4:2 says, "[Jonah] prayed to the LORD, 'Isn't this what I said, LORD, when I was still at home? That is what I tried to forestall by fleeing to Tarshish. I knew that you are a gracious and compassionate God, slow to anger and abounding in love, a God who relents from sending calamity.'"

Jonah ran not because he feared Nineveh's strength or his own failure, but because he was afraid of God's grace toward sinners.

Nineveh was the capital city of the Assyrian Empire, the greatest enemy of the people of Israel at that time. The Assyrians were a constant military threat to Jonah's homeland, and all of Israel despised and feared them. Jonah didn't want to go to Nineveh because he hated the city and its people. They were his enemies. He would have been thrilled to deliver a message of divine wrath against his enemies. To call down God's judgment against this empire would have been a massive win for Jonah and his people. What he feared was that his enemies would repent of their sins and God would show them grace. Jonah knew God's heart, and he would rather have seen his enemies wiped off the map than see them become his brothers and sisters through the mercy of Yahweh.

Do you ever fear God's grace toward sinners? Are you afraid he will mess up the lines that you have neatly drawn and reconfigure your categories for who is in and who is out of his favor? Are you afraid of what his grace toward sinners will demand of you?

Maintaining our neat categories and religious rules is not the same as obeying God. Condemning the people who hate God is not the same as loving God. We want prophets who will confront sin in the world. God often sends prophets to confront sin in the church. Are we listening?

HOW TO START A FIRE

After Jonah ran from God's call, God used a storm, a crew of pagan sailors, and a great fish to redirect Jonah's path. And "Jonah obeyed the word of the LORD and went to Nineveh" (Jon. 3:3). His trajectory was altered, and, in newly surrendered though begrudging obedience, Jonah walked into the heart of the enemy capital, preaching with authority.

What happened next was a miracle on par with a man being swallowed by a giant fish and living to talk about it. Jonah 3:5 says that the Ninevites believed God and repented of their sins. Even the king declared a collective fast and said, "Let everyone call urgently on God. Let them give up their evil ways and their violence. Who knows? God may yet relent and with compassion turn from his fierce anger so that we will not perish" (Jon. 3:8–9).

In his compassion, God forgave the people's sins, and a revival erupted in a city known for its wicked and violent opposition to the people and ways of Yahweh. The hearts of the Ninevites turned to God, and the city was transformed.

Doesn't this capture your imagination? Don't you want to see that happen in your city? Don't you pray for an awakening in your church, community, and country?

Jonah's story tells us that revival begins with repentance. We are altogether passionate about calling for repentance from the culture. We are happy to point out the ways sin "out there" is dismantling our society's character. In doing so we tragically miss the point. Nineveh's transformation did not start with an announcement from the king or mourning by the people. What was the spark that started this fire?

Nineveh's revival began with Jonah's repentance. Before the people were transformed, the prophet repented. He had run in the opposite direction, but then came a turn, a pivot, a reversal. There was a clear and unmistakable transformation in his direction based on an encounter with God. Before Nineveh could respond with obedience to God's voice, Jonah had to respond with obedience to God's voice. If we want to see repentance around us, it must begin with repentance within us. If you want others to repent, you must lead the way. You must repent first.

To repent means to turn. Jonah did just that. He changed direction. He faithfully proclaimed God's Word, even if he continued to harbor personal reservations. And his turning point became Nineveh's turning point. Confession is the catalyst for renewal as Christ is exalted in our humility.

When Jonah rolled into Nineveh and began to speak, he was a dead man resurrected. He was dead, taken down to the lowest depths. And then, by way of a miracle, he was raised back up. This is what Jesus referred to in Matthew 12 when he said that the only sign given to his own wicked generation would be the sign of Jonah—a dead man raised back to life. And God wants to give our generation the same sign. But for people to believe in the resurrection of Jesus, they need to see the resurrection of you.

We have been lulled into believing that spiritual renewal leading to social renewal simply can't happen in our day. We believe the lie that there is too much hostility toward our faith in the current culture for us to affect real change. That is a convenient line, but it's just not true. The greatest obstacle to revival is not a hostile environment in the culture but a culture of pride in the church. Which is more tragic, the person who has yet to realize his or her desperate need for grace or the person who has forgotten it? If we hope to see an awakening in our communities, it must begin with those of us who are asleep in the Light.

The church must lead the way in repentance if we are to see revival. But we often fail to see the two as intimately connected. In fact, we can see them as opposites. We believe repentance is about surrender and revival is about victory. One is for sinners, the other is for saints. Yet throughout Scripture, we find them tied together. Repentance is not a lever you can pull to bring about an instant change in the culture. Rather, humble and authentic repentance within the church is the prerequisite for revival, which will then produce a change in the culture. Only the heart of the Father, the love of the Son, and the power of the Holy Spirit initiate transformation in the world. And that begins with repentance in believers.

So, stop praying for revival in your church, community, and country unless you are willing to repent of your own spiritual pride. Stop declaring a week of revival in the church and begin by creating space for repentance in your own heart. Do not call for the culture to turn its heart back to God until you are willing to lead the way. Ask the Holy Spirit to examine your own heart and life, to reveal where you are wide of the mark, out of alignment, and on the run. And then, ask God to turn you back around.

THE NEXT BRAVE STEP

When we repent, we ask for forgiveness. Perhaps the only thing more difficult than asking for forgiveness is extending it to someone else. To risk forgiving a wrong runs against the pattern of our self-preserving instincts. But it is the next brave step.

We had to know this was coming. We understand that we can't follow Jesus and not practice what is at the core of his mission, purpose, teaching, actions, and heart. You cannot walk in the way of Jesus without tripping over the call to forgive. Forgiveness is something we are freely given and something we must freely give. It is our response to redemption. You've been forgiven. Who is next?

Understand, however, that there is a difference between forgiveness and trust. Forgiveness is given freely. Trust must be earned and, when broken, carefully and slowly rebuilt. Forgiveness can't be earned because it has already been paid for. And you didn't pay that price so you have no right to charge someone else for it.

Also, to forgive freely doesn't mean to do so easily or quickly or flippantly. We do not forgive as a way to get past a difficult situation. To forgive freely means to forgive extravagantly. This forgiveness overflows from a place of freedom—freedom so real and full and deep that it gives us the courage to free others. This cannot be done through our own power and courage but only through the power and courage of the cross. Forgiveness flows from the cross.

If forgiveness is to flow from a deep place of freedom in us, it will first require a season of healing in our own souls. This is something more than an immediate impulse. It may require a long and painful road of embracing that hurt head-on, wrestling with it, and pushing beyond it.

Healing our souls requires the brutal work of admitting and acknowledging our hurt. It requires us to look squarely at our natural, and at times healthy, anger. It forces us to identify what happened to us and acknowledge its impact. But healing our souls does not allow for holding on to the hurt or clutching our anger. It leads us through the hurt and anger to a point where we can surrender to the healing, release the hurt, and forgive.

You are allowed to hurt. You are allowed to be angry. But you must also be willing to be led through that season into the freedom of forgiveness. Again, it is a season, which means it's not always immediate, but neither is it permanent. It can't be allowed to persist forever. Even honest hurt and righteous anger that go unhealed will become seeds of bitterness, growing wild until they choke out the joy and hope and love of your life. In fact, that's what happened to Jonah. Even after preaching repentance to the Ninevites, he couldn't find it in his heart to forgive them. The end of this intriguing book finds Jonah sitting on a hillside, waiting for God to rain down judgment on the enemy. We don't know for sure whether Jonah's heart ever softened or if he remained in that place of joyless anger. But since we have this book, written under his own name, we assume he did. Perhaps this book itself is a form of written repentance, confessing his failure for the world to see. And at the same time challenging each reader to honestly repent and freely forgive.

Following Jesus leads us through the wilderness of hurt and anger, down twisting trails, and along narrow ledges, until, finally, we are guided into the clearing of forgiveness. Our instincts tell us we are going the wrong way, that this can't be right. But the compass is clear, and the way of Jesus is marked by selfless action against our instinct to withhold forgiveness. Forgiveness is the undeniable sign of the Father's unrivaled reign in your life; of the power and courage of the cross flowing from you; of the Holy Spirit's work of resurrection and new creation in your soul. Forgiveness is the way of Jesus. Repentance is the infrastructure of revival. And repentance begins with you.

6

OLD & NEW

Let's be honest. As Christians we often don't know exactly what to do with the Old Testament. It records events that took place in foreign cultural settings and contains confusing laws and customs and, often, troubling actions and declarations. It seems entirely different from the New Testament, where God's love and grace take center stage. To resolve the tension, we simply draw a line across the pages of history and embrace the New Testament while ignoring the Old. It's not that we reject the Old Testament; we just keep it at a safe distance.

Dr. Sandra Richter reminds us that the Old Testament is not "'the unfortunate preface' to the part of the Bible that really matters."[1] And this is our story. It's time for us to step into our whole story again and walk back through the roots of redemption. In this chapter, we explore the paradox that holds the old and new covenants together by wrestling through three key questions:

- Why does God seem different from the Old Testament to the New Testament?
- How do the Old and New Testaments relate to each other?
- Why do the Old and New Testaments appear to contradict each other?

Christians and skeptics alike debate these questions. You've probably asked them yourself. So let's face them head-on and dive in with the first question.

WHY DOES GOD SEEM DIFFERENT FROM THE OLD TO NEW TESTAMENTS?

Jesus didn't come to announce that God had changed. He came to announce that everything we've ever known about God has been fulfilled, revealed, and made clear in himself. Jesus didn't distance himself from the old covenant or from the God of Israel. Rather, he tied himself to the old covenant and identified himself by means of it.

God hasn't changed. Jesus' coming to earth wasn't a last-ditch effort to save the world because the other things God had tried didn't work. God's plan was always Jesus. Every covenant he made with his people pointed ahead and prepared the way for Christ; Jesus himself reinforced that idea with unswerving clarity.

When Jesus launched his ministry, Luke said he did so by quoting an Old Testament prophecy from Isaiah 61. In his hometown synagogue, Jesus stood to read from this passage, then claimed it as the framework for his mission. The ancient promise delivered through Isaiah hadn't changed. Rather, it continued and swelled to fulfillment in Christ (see Luke 4:16–21).

Later, on an isolated mountaintop, Jesus was transfigured before his inner circle of disciples and was revealed in his blinding glory. At that moment, old covenant luminaries Moses and Elijah flanked him on either side. In Jesus' day, the sacred Scriptures were often referred to as the Law and the Prophets. In this moment of transfiguration, Moses, who delivered the law, and Elijah, the greatest of the prophets, gave reverence to Jesus—because Jesus is the completion of both ministries. Moses and Elijah, like the books of the Law and the Prophets, direct our attention to Jesus, the centerpiece of Scripture (see Luke 9:28–31).

After Jesus' resurrection, he appeared to a few of his disciples as they walked along a road. They didn't recognize him and filled him in on the devastating events that had recently taken place: Their beloved Jesus had been crucified and his grave had been found empty. How did Jesus break through their despair and teach them what had really happened? He taught them from the Old Testament: "And beginning with Moses and all the Prophets, he explained to them what was said in all the Scriptures concerning himself" (Luke 24:25–27). Although Jesus pioneered this new resurrection life, he began his teaching by pointing back, drawing their hearts and minds to ancient roots. Even this watershed moment that disrupted reality as we know it, declares that God has not changed. He is simply continuing to be himself. As

A. W. Tozer said, "'What is God like?' A proper answer will always be, 'He is like Christ.' For Christ is God, and the man who walked among men in Palestine was God acting like himself."[2]

HOW DO THE OLD AND NEW TESTAMENTS RELATE TO EACH OTHER?

The relationship between the Old and New Testaments is similar to the relationship between John the Baptist and Jesus—one prepares the way for the other. As the gospel of John begins, we immediately see that the author was trying to spark our memory. The first three words of his gospel are "In the beginning." Where have we heard that before? The book of Genesis begins the exact same way. John's original audience would have made the connection immediately. The story of Jesus is a new creation moment. What went wrong in the old story of Genesis 3 will be set right in this new story. The creation narrative points ahead to Jesus and his mission.

In John 2, we see that Jesus performed his first miracle by turning water into wine at a wedding. Interestingly, Jesus told the servants at the wedding to fill six stone jars with water. These jars were normally used for ceremonial cleansing, preparing for the people to worship. Jesus transformed the water in these jars, and when the people tasted this new wine they said, "You have saved the best till now" (John 2:10). The old purpose points ahead, then steps aside for the new and better.

Keep looking. What happens next in the gospel of John? Jesus cleansed the temple. The other three gospels place this controversial moment at the end of Jesus' ministry, framing this event as a catalyst for his trial and crucifixion. Yet John placed this story right up front. Why? Because John didn't structure his gospel in chronological order. Rather, he grouped together stories according to theme or meaningful connection. What is the theme and connection? Once again, it's the old way, the temple, pointing ahead to the new way, Jesus—the very living presence of Yahweh. As Jesus was indicating in his conversation with the Samaritan woman at the well (see John 4), the historic, place-centered spirit of worship had been preparing the way for worship of God in "Spirit and in truth" (John 4:23), that is, with the Spirit of God in the worshiper.

The author was not done yet. We meet Nicodemus, the famous Pharisee who was irresistibly drawn to the character of Jesus (John 3). Once again, we have the juxtaposed images of the religious leader, a guardian and champion of the old, and Jesus, the embodiment of the new.

The entire section climaxes with the act of John the Baptist. The text speaks for itself:

> They came to John and said to him, "Rabbi, that man who was with you on the other side of the Jordan—the one you testified about—look, he is baptizing, and everyone is going to him." To this John replied, "A person can receive only what is given them from heaven. You yourselves can testify that I said, 'I am not the Messiah but am sent ahead

of him." The bride belongs to the bridegroom. The friend who attends the bridegroom waits and listens for him, and is full of joy when he hears the bridegroom's voice. That joy is mine, and it is now complete. He must become greater; I must become less." (John 3:26–30)

And there it is. Like John the Baptist, the Old Testament points ahead and prepares the way for Jesus. The life of Jesus is the most crucial lens for understanding and viewing the Old Testament. And the old covenant is a crucial lens for understanding the full significance of Jesus. Always remember, without immersing yourself in the rich truth of the Old Testament, you will continue to miss meaningful layers to the Jesus story.

WHY DO THE OLD AND NEW TESTAMENTS APPEAR TO CONTRADICT EACH OTHER?

We must be genuine and acknowledge that many parts of Scripture are hard to reconcile with one another. We must always be honest about our questions and never ignore them and be kind toward others who are wrestling with Scripture. Never dismiss or downplay sincere questions and doubt. God welcomes them because they can lead you to deeper faith. There is ample room in our faith for asking questions.

Yet as we pull back and look at the larger picture, we discover that what we first see as contradictions form a mosaic of connections.

When we lean in closely and examine carefully, we discover that they do not contradict each other but are in conversation, even completing each other's sentences.

The Old Testament is not an odd collection of barbaric stories and archaic rules. It is the sweeping narrative of God's active redemption of the world. It is salvation history. Don't ignore the questions, but let the connections shed light on how you see the story.

The common critique is that the God of the Old Testament is full of wrath and judgment, while the God of the New Testament is full of love and grace. If this is true, then it is clearly a troubling contradiction, suggesting that the Bible does not present a cohesive vision of God's character.

At first glance, it's easy to understand this confusion. The Old Testament contains many difficult-to-stomach stories that involve God's wrath upon sin. And critics of the Bible who have little grasp of the larger narrative consistently point to these moments as evidence that God's character is changeable or untrustworthy.

But clear patterns of God's consistent character run throughout the Old Testament. Even the moments of wrath reveal God's grace. Grace in a catastrophic flood? Grace in the fire and brimstone of Sodom and Gomorrah? Grace in the military destruction of Jericho? Yes, each of these accounts demonstrate the just consequences for people living in open rebellion against God. Yet in each case it is clear that God, in his rich grace, offered an opportunity to be saved. Noah's family, Lot and his daughters, and Rahab the prostitute each stand as witnesses to a truth that ties together the Old and New Testaments in a cohesive whole: Sin must be judged, but God always offers rescue.

As we examine the sweep of the Old Testament, we can see that God's grace abounds in the creation narrative as he formed humanity in his own image; in Abraham's story as he blessed the entire world through two people too old to have children; in the exodus as he sent Moses to deliver Israel from slavery in Egypt; in David's life as he raised up the least likely servant to become the anointed shepherd king.

And of course the New Testament depicts God's unchanging judgment against sin. Never forget that the most gut-wrenching image of God's wrath and judgment in the entire Bible is in the cross, where he took the wrath and judgment upon himself. The old collides with the new, bound together by paradox. The Bible is still alive and moving in the hearts of God's people, shaping us for the sake of the world. This is our story. All of it. And as we seek to understand and experience it, let us faithfully live it in empowered response.

ONE LAST CHALLENGE

Thirst for knowledge. Study and research the reliability of Scripture. Wrestle with these questions and more. A true, robust faith is not afraid of the searching. But remember that there comes a time when the searching gives way to finding. Asking leads to an invitation to know and respond. For many, these questions have been settled. If that describes you, then your life is no longer defined by the question of Scripture's reliability but by the question of your response.

In our day we have the deepest thoughts of the brightest theologians collected in our pockets. We have great knowledge. Yet we may fail to do anything about what we know. We have a wealth of information and a poverty of obedience. The entire scope of Scripture, the old and new together, calls us to walk in active obedience and engagement with the Living Word.

What about you? How will you respond? What will you do with the knowledge you've been given?

NOTES

1. Sandra Richter, *The Epic of Eden: A Christian Entry into the Old Testament* (Downers Grove, IL: InterVarsity Press, 2008), 16.
2. A. W. Tozer, *God's Pursuit of Man* (Chicago: Moody, 1978), n.p.

7

INDIVIDUALITY & COMMUNITY

Christianity is a personal faith. It calls for each individual to receive salvation by grace through faith in Jesus. No one can make that decision for another. No one can surrender another person's life or be obedient, rescued, or transformed on behalf of someone else. We do not inherit salvation based on culture, social connections, or bloodlines. The saving love of Jesus is deeply personal, penetrates the soul, and has a radical impact on every aspect of who we are. The call to "Come, follow me" demands a personal response.

As such, it is right for us to emphasize personal growth in the grace of Jesus. Each believer must surrender to the Holy Spirit and live in a rich relationship with the Father. Personal prayer, Scripture reading, and cultivating the inner life are crucial parts of this Christian journey.

But in our culture, where rugged individualism is a cardinal virtue and the self-made success story is our civic myth, it is crucial to tell the other side of the story. Life in Christ is also a collective experience. We each are part of a family, a movement, a kingdom. The blood of Jesus unites us with believers across time and around the world. Christian faith is both personal and collective.

CREATED FOR RELATIONSHIP

Think about your very first friend. Chances are, you'll have to reach back pretty far to find that memory. There is something deep within us that is drawn to others. We are wired for relationship. It is embedded in our DNA, a mark that makes us human.

But the desire for connection didn't begin at your beginning. You can trace its history all the way back to creation. In all of the poetic creation narrative, there is only one thing God says is not good: for Adam to be alone. We are made for relationship with each other.

Let's reach even further back. Our hunger for connection actually predates creation. We have a primal longing for relationship because we are created in God's image. And God exists in relationship for all eternity. Christians are monotheists because we believe in the one true God. And we are Trinitarian because we believe that the one God exists as three persons. God is God the Father, God the Son, and God the Holy Spirit—the Holy Trinity, the all-divine three in one. God exists in unbreakable relationship within himself, and we are designed to be caught up in the holy love that fires between three persons in one. And as bearers of God's image, we are made for relationship with each other.

COMMUNITY IS SACRED

The life of King David demonstrates the power of both the individual and community. Although David failed in many ways, he was known for his loyalty in friendships and dedication not just to God but to God's people as well. David's relationship with God was intimate and personal, as revealed by the Psalms. And he also recognized his need to share his journey with covenant friends. Enter the legendary mighty men. This brotherhood of soldiers fought with and for David through many of his darkest moments and greatest victories. They were courageous and heroic warriors, yet we remember them for their tender loyalty and friendship. One story is found in 2 Samuel 23:13–17:

> During harvest time, three of the thirty chief warriors came down to David at the cave of Adullam, while a band of Philistines was encamped in the Valley of Rephaim. At that time David was in the stronghold, and the Philistine garrison was at Bethlehem. David longed for water and said, "Oh, that someone would get me a drink of water from the well near the gate of Bethlehem!" So the three mighty warriors broke through the Philistine lines, drew water from the well near the gate of Bethlehem and carried it back to David. But he refused to drink it; instead, he poured it out before the Lord. "Far be it from me, Lord, to do this!" he said. "Is it not the blood of men who went at the risk of their lives?" And David would not drink it.

At first glance, it may seem like an act of reckless disrespect for David to pour out the water on the ground. It might appear that he wasted the sacrifice made by his courageous friends. But this was no act of disrespect. It was an act of reverence. He honored his friends' sacrifice by refusing to quench his thirst with water that could have cost their lives.

And there is more. As we see this event in the context of Israel's covenant relationship with Yahweh and the worship practices he established through Moses, a new layer emerges. You may know of the concept of burnt offerings—an animal sacrificed on an altar and burned. This is perhaps the most common image of Old Testament worship. But there were other forms of sacrifice as well, including the drink offering. At times, worshipers poured out wine before God as a gift. This passage says that David took the water and "poured it out before the LORD." David took the gift offered by his friends and offered it in worship to God.

Friendship is sacred. Love is sacrifice. Community is worship. This sacrifice by David was both an act of love toward his friends and an act of worship toward God.

In response to grace, in response to the extravagant, poured-out love of Jesus toward us, we pour out our love toward others. Remember once again the Great Commandment Jesus gave us. We are called to love God with all we have and all we are, and to love others in the same reckless way. We must do both or we do neither. An act of love toward another is an act of worship toward God.

COMMUNITY IS CREATED THROUGH STRUGGLE

It's interesting that the bonds of friendship between David and his mighty men were forged in the throes of battle, because community is something we have to fight for. Authentic Christian community is empowered by the unifying presence of the Holy Spirit, but it still requires selflessness, sacrifice, and struggle on our part. We claim to want community. We say we love it. But if we're honest, we probably love the ideal more than the messy, difficult, long road toward the thing itself. The harsh truth is if we are not willing to fight for community, we will never experience it.

Proverbs 27:17 gives us a popular image of and call toward authentic community, and for good reason. "As iron sharpens iron," it says, "so one person sharpens another." But this brilliant imagery is more dangerous than we first realize because it promises that community will create friction. In the painful friction of one piece of iron moving against another, both are refined. Community emerges from the motion of life-to-life contact. Friendships are forged and shaped by the friction between us.

Friction is inevitable when humans share space. And we often bail when we feel that burn and miss the opportunity for relationships to take shape. Conflict is not part of the ideal community we have imagined, so when it occurs we assume the relationship isn't working and give up. But friction doesn't have to cause division. It can be harnessed to sharpen individuals and communities, pushing us closer to our potential. Who are the "iron" friends who sharpen your soul?

In Proverbs 27:6, we see that friction can come in the form of wounds from a friend. "Wounds from a friend can be trusted, but an enemy multiplies kisses." At first glance, this doesn't sound like fighting for a relationship but fighting against it. What kind of friend inflicts wounds? But this text does not refer to betrayal or undercutting. This is about building up, not breaking down. There is a difference between hurting and harming.

A genuine friend will tell you what you need to hear, not what you want to hear. True friends will bear your momentary anger for the sake of your long-term good. Dietrich Bonhoeffer warned us that sin wants us alone, isolated and cut off from community.[1] So resist the temptation to reject the truth from friends, even when it hurts. Don't pull back and isolate yourself. Discern their motivation, hear their hearts, and determine if there is any helpful correction in the hard truth. Like a good surgeon, a friend is willing to wound you for the sake of healing you.

An enemy, however, will prop up your weaknesses and never force you to make adjustments. Enemies will not stand in your way when you're on the wrong path because they do not care where you end up. They have no interest in your true condition because they have no investment in you. A friend has skin in the game. A friend will speak hard truth. Friends are willing to endure the burn of friction to see you shine like sharpened iron.

So don't bail on a relationship when you feel the friction. Lean into the sharpening. Embrace the opportunity. It is significant that this story of David and his mighty men took place in a cave, not a coffee shop. Community is something you must fight for.

COMMUNITY IS CULTIVATED OVER TIME

One line in this story bears a second look. It's the opening phrase "during harvest time" (2 Sam. 23:13). That seemingly insignificant detail about the season of the year sparks an interesting thought. This is not scriptural exposition, just an observation: Community becomes evident during harvest time. In other words, community must be cultivated. It takes time. We must repeat the familiar pattern of plowing and planting before we can see the harvest. No farmer walks into the field one morning and stumbles upon a harvest. Only after months of careful cultivation does the farmer see the plants push up through the ground and finally ripen to a harvest. And just because the farmer enjoyed a great harvest last year does not mean there will automatically be an abundant one this year. Community is never automatic. It requires the sweat and pain of breaking hard ground, planting seeds beneath the surface, tending them through the growth process, and being patient while the harvest matures.

There is a rhythm to the harvest. You must submit to the process by putting in the hard work of cultivating if you want to experience the joy of community. This sounds simple, but it is not easy. We often fall into one of three roles when it comes to building authentic Christian community. First is the critic, who asks, "What is wrong?" Second is the consumer, who asks, "What's here for me?" Third is the creator, who asks, "What can I do?" Ironically, you must be all three in order to see the harvest of community. You need to critique, to see the gaps where growth is needed and to care enough to speak up. And you must consume by receiving the benefits of community by having a mentor or group of people who pour themselves into you and your spiritual life. But the critic and consumer stages must not be the end. You must go on to become a creator as well. When you see that something isn't what it needs to be, don't just talk about it. Become part of the solution. Are you concerned with your own needs? Chances are good that others need the same things. Dig in and help pass on what you have received to the next person. Don't just be a critic or a consumer. Become a creator. Cultivate a harvest of authentic community.

THE POWER OF COMMUNITY

Scientists have discovered a fascinating trait about fire ants. They cannot swim, and a single fire ant alone will drown in water within seconds. But these creatures have an incredible instinctual reaction when threatened by a flood. Sensing the danger, fire ants flock to each other and lock their tiny legs and jaws together. They connect so tightly that their joined bodies create an air-tight raft that enables them to float across the water's surface. Thousands of interlocked fire ants can survive a disastrous flood, floating together for weeks at a time. Together, they survive the flood. Yet a single ant broken apart from the group will drown.[2]

These incredible creatures dramatically illustrate the power of community. Alone, we drown in a flood of negative forces from our culture. Together, we survive. If you have a friend who is facing the flood, rush to his or her side. Link arms with your friend and you will both gain strength as you lean on each other.

A NEW COMMAND

Centuries after King David lived, another anointed Shepherd-King cast the vision of authentic community. With some of Jesus' last words to his disciples, he planted the seed of unity in the upstart movement that would bear his name. And they needed it. In fact, they failed to live up to that vision even before they finished dinner. By the end of the evening, Peter had denied knowing Jesus and the others had scattered, running for the shadows. Yet they all sat around the table of Jesus' last supper and listened to these words: "A new command I give you: Love one another. As I have loved you, so you must love one another" (John 13:34).

In what way was this a new command? It was a new command because of the scope and character of the love that would be required to carry it out. Jesus' earlier command was to love others "as yourself" (Matt. 22:39). The new command was to love others "as I have loved you" (John 13:34). And how had Jesus loved? He responded to hurt with grace. He answered betrayal by washing feet. He foresaw denial and countered it with premeditated friendship. "If you will love each other like this," Jesus taught his disciples, "the world will know that you are mine."

Jesus invites us to follow him into an intimate relationship and personal faith. But on his last night with his friends he reminded them that they were not meant to walk the road alone. Christianity is an individual response to Jesus Christ. And it is a collective faith. The world will know we are Jesus' disciples by the way we love one another.

NOTES

1. Dietrich Bonhoeffer, *Life Together*, trans. John W. Doberstein (San Francisco: Harper & Row, 1954), 112.

2. Brian Clark Howard, "How Ants Survive Flooding by Forming Giant Rafts," *National Geographic*, October 6, 2015, http://news.nationalgeographic.com/2015/10/151006-fire-ants-rafts-south-carolina-flooding/.

8

HOLINESS & LOVE

How would you complete the following statement? God is _____. Many possible descriptions may come to mind. God is good, sovereign, glorious, powerful, great, mighty. We could continue that list until we exhaust our vocabulary, yet even then we wouldn't have begun to describe God. No single term can define his character.

However, two terms seem to push their way to the front when we think of God. They emerge in our minds because they are buried in our memory. Throughout Scripture, God is revealed, described, worshiped, and proclaimed by these two ideas: God is holy, and God is love.

God is holy means that he is other, that is, set apart, different, far off; and it means that God is pure, meaning uncorrupted, perfect, sinless. As a result, God's holiness makes him entirely unapproachable. He is infinitely above and beyond us. To prove that, we need only look at the moments when he did come close to human beings. Throughout the Bible, when God spoke or when he revealed even a portion of his glory to humans, the reaction was the same—sheer terror. They collapsed in utter fear, convinced they were about to die. When God was about to speak to Moses in the wilderness, we read, "When the people saw the thunder and lightning and heard the trumpet and saw the mountain in smoke, they trembled with fear. They stayed at a distance and said to Moses, 'Speak to us yourself and we will listen. But do not have God speak to us or we will die'" (Ex. 20:18–19). Suddenly it becomes clear how completely other God is. These beings of dust and breath know they cannot hope to stand in his presence for even a moment. They brace for death, preparing to be crushed beneath the weight of his glory.

Yet, as many of these same encounters with God recorded in Scripture make clear, God is also love, and he does draw close to his people. Though he doesn't need us, God consistently shows that he wants a relationship with us. The unapproachable approaches us. The Most High descends. Yes, we should tremble in fear and wonder at his holiness. Yet from Abraham and Moses to Isaiah and Elijah, God has consistently reached out to his creation in personal ways. So we are left with this paradox: the holy, unapproachable God, whose presence is too awesome to withstand, desires personal, intimate contact with us, who are weak and sinful human beings. God is holy; God is love. Both are somehow true.

For help navigating between these core attributes of God, we turn to the book of Hebrews, where both strands of God's character are held together in one place: the person of Jesus Christ.

JESUS SURPASSES ALL

Written to Jewish Christians during a time of intense persecution, the purpose of Hebrews was to strengthen believers during trials. They were experiencing far more than negative social pressure or changing cultural values; these believers lived every day under the threat of death. Some scholars believe Hebrews was written soon after the deaths of Peter and Paul, the catalytic leaders of the upstart Christian movement. Pressure mounted from all sides for these Christians to return to their roots in Judaism or renounce Jesus altogether as a means of escaping death. The writer of Hebrews employed compelling rhetoric to plead with his readers to not shrink back, arguing that Jesus is worth it. He encouraged, motivated, and warned. He used inspiration, theology, history, and logic all to make one single point—Jesus is greater than anything that has come before. He said:

- Jesus is greater than their history because he is eternal.
- Jesus is greater than the patriarchs because he is the source of all life.
- Jesus is greater than the covenants because he completes them.
- Jesus is greater than the law because he fulfills it.
- Jesus is greater than the prophets because he is the living Word of God.
- Jesus is greater than the monarchy because he will reign above all things forever.

- Jesus is greater than the priests because he is the object of our worship.
- Jesus is greater than the high priests because he is the once-and-for-all sacrifice that brings full atonement for sin.

After all this, the preacher escalated his rhetoric even further to make this astounding claim: Jesus is even greater than the temple because he gives us full access to God.

Look at his stunning words in Hebrews 10:19–23:

Therefore, brothers and sisters, since we have confidence to enter the Most Holy Place by the blood of Jesus, by a new and living way opened for us through the curtain, that is, his body, and since we have a great priest over the house of God, let us draw near to God with a sincere heart and with the full assurance that faith brings, having our hearts sprinkled to cleanse us from a guilty conscience and having our bodies washed with pure water. Let us hold unswervingly to the hope we profess, for he who promised is faithful.

HOLY SEPARATION

This was a wild statement to make to an audience with deep Jewish roots. They understood that in the temple, God literally dwelled among the people. The unapproachable, untouchable, Most High God localized himself by enthroning his presence within the four walls of that building. That concept had its origins in the founding event of the kingdom of Israel, the exodus. After leaving the slavery of Egypt, God's people wandered through the wilderness before entering the Promised Land. During that wandering, God instructed Moses to make for him a tent called the tabernacle. In this portable structure, God would literally take up residence with his people as they lived in the desert. Centuries later, the permanent temple, built in the spiritual and political capital of Jerusalem, reflected the same basic design of the tabernacle, though on a different scale.

The temple was laid out in several sections, each layer becoming more holy and restricted than the one before. The outer section was the court of the Gentiles, and it was open to anyone. Next was the court of the women, which was open only to Jews. After that was the court of Israel, which could be entered only by Jewish men who were bringing their sacrifices or participating in the rituals and practices prescribed by God to Moses. Only a select few were allowed to venture beyond these courts.

Within the walls of the temple was a smaller, more restricted space called the Holy Place. The average Jewish worshiper could never step foot inside this sacred environment. Only the priests could enter. And to become a priest, you had to be born in the right family line—only descendants of Aaron were eligible. Everyone in that culture understood that this restricted access reflected the holiness of God. These barriers were established and observed to honor the purity of God and to protect the people. Every time a priest left the courts and entered into the Holy Place, this message was etched deeper in the Jewish mind-set: God is holy.

But there was still another space, even more sacred and therefore more restricted. Within the Holy Place there was a smaller section called the Most Holy Place. It was divided even from the Holy Place by a curtain symbolizing the separation of a Most Holy God from sinful humanity. Behind that veil lived the very presence of God himself, enthroned in glory and might among his people.

The Most Holy Place was so revered that not even the priests could pass behind the curtain. This space was so surpassingly sacred that only one person could enter, and then on only one day per year. This singular person was the high priest, selected by God for that year to make one sacrifice on behalf of all of the people. One person, one sacrifice, for all of the people. When he entered the Most Holy Place, the high priest wore bells on his clothing and a rope around his ankle so that if he did not survive this encounter with God the priests outside the curtain would know because the bells stopped ringing and then they could drag him out using the rope. That's how seriously the Jewish people took God's holiness.

LOVING RECONCILIATION

In light of this context, the words in Hebrews 10:19–23 are even more incredible. Read them again with fresh eyes:

> Therefore, brothers and sisters, since we have confidence to
> enter the Most Holy Place by the blood of Jesus, by a new

and living way opened for us through the curtain, that is, his body, and since we have a great priest over the house of God, let us draw near to God with a sincere heart and with the full assurance that faith brings, having our hearts sprinkled to cleanse us from a guilty conscience and having our bodies washed with pure water. Let us hold unswervingly to the hope we profess, for he who promised is faithful.

God is holy and cannot be approached. And God is love that cannot be contained. Because God is holy, sin must be judged. And because God is love, he took that judgment upon himself. Jesus became the once-and-for-all sacrifice for our sins. His broken body destroyed the barrier, opening for us a passage into God's presence.

Remember that the temple was a mere shadow of things to come. Jesus is the reality. That's why, when Jesus died on the cross, the veil in the temple that separated the Holy Place from the Most Holy Place was torn in two from top to bottom (see Matt. 27:51). His blood paid the penalty for our sin and brought us back to God.

There's more. Acts 2 tells us that on the day of Pentecost, for the first time in history all believers were filled with the living presence of God through the Holy Spirit. That means not only can we now enter God's presence, but God also enters us. We become walking temples, carrying the presence of God within us. God has sent his holy, loving presence into this broken world through you and me.

Ernest Hemingway said, "The world breaks everyone," and he was right.[1] We all have the scars to prove it. Every day we see and experience suffering and injustice, unmistakable signs of the sin that dominates our fallen world. The sharp edges of brokenness are everywhere. But brokenness is not the end of the story. Because the Holy Spirit dwells in us, we are living, breathing demonstrations of holy love. As we come alive in Christ, we come awake to our purpose, and God's ancient promise echoes in our souls. We have a hope, a future, a plan, a calling. Through a unique convergence of gifts and passions, God expresses his holiness and his love to the world through us. This is the genius of God: He plants himself in each of us so we become an extension of his mission in the world. Everywhere we go, the kingdom rolls out beneath our feet, claiming new ground with each bold step. We are the called ones, sent on a mission to become sparks of redemption, fighting back the shadows of the fall wherever we find them. Our lives become signal flares against the night, burning brightly to light the way.

CLOSE ENCOUNTERS

Think about what that means for you and the opportunities you face every day. When those students step into your class on the first day of school, they have the potential to experience an encounter with the living God, alive in you. When patients step into your clinic, customers walk up to your counter, people stand next to you in line, strangers sit next to you on the bus, or coworkers engage you in the break room or boardroom, they are dangerously close to an all-out transformational encounter with the holy, loving God.

When you're attacked by an enemy or betrayed by a friend, you are empowered to respond with a reckless love that can come from only one source: the living God, alive in you. When you lay down your head at night, perhaps frightened and alone, that very spot becomes the majestic palace of the Most High God, alive in you.

And we carry this message wherever we go. Are you tired? He will give you rest. Are you hurting? He will heal you. Are you discouraged? He will lift your head. Are you afraid? He will go before you. Are you uncertain? He will never fail. Are you trapped? He is freedom. Are you at a dead end? He is the new and living way.

Because God is holy, sin must be judged. And because God is love, he took that judgment upon himself, becoming the once-and-for-all sacrifice, opening the way for us to enter his presence. Because God is holy, he cannot be approached. And because God is love, he came near to us. He fills our hearts with holy love and drives us out, unleashed to mend the broken places in our world.

NOTE

1. Ernest Hemingway, *A Farewell to Arms* (New York: Scribner, 1997), 226.

9

FAITH & WORKS

Martin Luther was an instigator, a trouble-making friar whose rebellion pushed the Roman Catholic Church toward reformation. For that, we honor him. Protesting the unbiblical practice of selling indulgences, which promised that a monetary gift to a charitable fund could purchase the favor of God, Luther wrote his watershed Ninety-Five Theses. This extensive list laid out, point by point, why this practice was not only unbiblical but also completely opposite of God's character. When Luther nailed this protest document to the door of the church in Wittenberg, Germany, on October 31, 1517, a groundswell of change was set in motion.

Luther and others continued to protest the errors and abuses of the Roman Catholic Church, stressing the supremacy of scriptural truth over church dogma. In particular, Luther reclaimed the biblical truth that salvation comes by grace alone through faith alone in Christ alone.

Luther was excommunicated by Pope Leo X, then tried for heresy. With his life on the line, Luther was given one last opportunity to recant his beliefs and be spared. "Here I stand," he answered. "I can do no other."[1] He was convicted and declared an outlaw by the Holy Roman Empire.

Luther was being escorted from the court hearings when his transport was hijacked. As it turns out, the hijackers were supporters sent to rescue him. They carried him to safety where he continued to write about the free gift of God's grace, the heart of the gospel message. Luther translated the Bible from Latin into German, preached against the abuses of religious power, and helped push forward what we call the Protestant Reformation.

Today, those of us who call ourselves Protestants continue that protest, proclaiming the countercultural good news of salvation by grace. Salvation cannot be earned, not by tossing coins into an offering plate or by piling up good works. Salvation is the free gift of God's grace, made available through faith in Jesus. No amount of effort can achieve that for us. No behavior can earn it or keep it. There is boundless freedom in that truth. Salvation is not something you do for God; it is what God has done for you.

The tension here, hence the paradox, is the relationship that we intuitively know should exist between salvation and righteousness. If there is no such thing as salvation by works—and there isn't—then are works unimportant? In other words, if you're not saved by the things you do, does your behavior matter? For centuries, Christians have gravitated toward one pole or the other on this paradox. Some wish to make our good actions all-important, which results in legalism, the idea that our right actions are proof of our righteousness before God. Others view behavior as meaningless, which results in licentiousness, a permissive form of faith in which "anything goes." The truth is found in the tension between faith and works.

FAITH NOT WORKS

Martin Luther's teaching was not new. It was at the core of the life and ministry of the apostle Paul. As chief theologian of the New Testament, Paul knew firsthand the power of grace to rescue and restore a hopeless sinner. His theology matched his biography. Paul began his career as a religious perfectionist and Jewish zealot who persecuted Christians to their deaths. Then Paul had a life-changing encounter with the resurrected Jesus. The very man who had once determined to crush Christianity became its most effective missionary, spreading the grace he had received to everyone he met. Paul's deeply personal conversion experience drove his eloquent defense of the power of grace.

In Ephesians 2:4–9, he captured the message this way:

But because of his great love for us, God, who is rich in mercy, made us alive with Christ even when we were dead in transgressions—it is by grace you have been saved. And God raised us up with Christ and seated us with him in the heavenly realms in Christ Jesus, in order that in the coming ages he might show the incomparable riches of his grace, expressed in his kindness to us in Christ Jesus. For it is by grace you have been saved, through faith—and this is not from yourselves, it is the gift of God—not by works, so that no one can boast.

Salvation cannot be won through our good works, no matter how good those works might be. Christ alone can save, and without his life we are dead in sin. As John Wesley said, "Only the power that makes a world can make a Christian."[2]

To demonstrate how ridiculous it is to boast about our good works, Paul referred to his own religious track record—which was astounding—as amounting to nothing (see Phil. 3:8). Paul had spent his life building a stellar résumé, learning under the most respected mentors, climbing the ranks of the religious elite. Yet he realized all that effort was worth nothing compared to the surpassing greatness of Christ. Borrowing from the descriptive language of Isaiah 64, where the prophet compared righteous acts done without sincerity to filthy rags, Paul went a step further. He referred to his good works as excrement. Often translated as "garbage" or "refuse," the actual Greek term used is likely a harsh reference to animal dung. It dramatically makes the point that your own good deeds are a vulgar and detestable substitute for God's grace. To depend on your own merits for salvation is misplaced trust, and misplaced trust is idolatry. There simply is no such thing as salvation by works. Insisting that people "prove themselves" to God by behaving well enough to merit salvation is unbiblical, unfaithful, and harmful to hurting people.

FAITH WITHOUT WORKS

If good works are not needed for salvation, then why does our behavior matter at all? What difference does it make what we do if God has already extended his mercy to us through the sacrifice of Jesus? The answer is that while living a good life doesn't produce saving faith, saving faith does result in a changed heart and life. Good works should flow from authentic faith.

Let's dig into that idea by looking at James 2:14–24. Many scholars point to this passage as an opposing take on Paul's theology of faith alone. They pit Paul and James against each other in heated debate over the nature of faith and works. Some even select these two passages as proof that the Bible is riddled with contradictions. Read for yourself and see what you think.

> What good is it, my brothers and sisters, if someone claims to have faith but has no deeds? Can such faith save them? Suppose a brother or a sister is without clothes and daily food. If one of you says to them, "Go in peace; keep warm and well fed," but does nothing about their physical needs, what good is it? In the same way, faith by itself, if it is not accompanied by action, is dead. But someone will say, "You have faith; I have deeds." Show me your faith without deeds, and I will show you my faith by my deeds. You believe that there is one God. Good! Even the demons believe that—and shudder. You foolish person, do you want evidence that faith without deeds is useless? Was not our father

Abraham considered righteous for what he did when he offered his son Isaac on the altar? You see that his faith and his actions were working together, and his faith was made complete by what he did. And the scripture was fulfilled that says, "Abraham believed God, and it was credited to him as righteousness," and he was called God's friend. You see that a person is considered righteous by what they do and not by faith alone.

Do you feel the tension here? Good. You should feel it. Is this a contradiction within the New Testament? Is this James versus Paul? Not at all. James was not saying that good works create saving faith. Rather, he was saying that a living faith never fails to produce good works. A vibrant faith will naturally produce obedience to God. If your faith is not producing that, then your faith is dead. Actually, you have no faith at all.

Both Paul and James wrote to correct dangerous misunderstandings. Paul addressed those who believed their good works would save them. James wrote to those who thought their right answers would save them. Both writers appealed to Abraham to make seemingly opposite points. But there is no contradiction here; there is connection.

Paul, writing to those who thought their good works were enough to save them, highlighted Abraham's faith. James, writing to those who used their theological knowledge as a hypocritical excuse to avoid helping others, highlighted the way Abraham's faith produced a life of stellar obedience. If you're still not convinced, return to Paul's words in Ephesians 2, that beautiful treatise on salvation by faith alone. Why go back now? Because we didn't actually finish the passage. We left out verse 10, presented here in italics.

> But because of his great love for us, God, who is rich in mercy, made us alive with Christ even when we were dead in transgressions—it is by grace you have been saved. And God raised us up with Christ and seated us with him in the heavenly realms in Christ Jesus, in order that in the coming ages he might show the incomparable riches of his grace, expressed in his kindness to us in Christ Jesus. For it is by grace you have been saved, through faith—and this is not from yourselves, it is the gift of God—not by works, so that no one can boast. *For we are God's handiwork, created in Christ Jesus to do good works, which God prepared in advance for us to do.* (Eph. 2:4–10, emphasis added)

There is no contradiction between Paul and James—or between faith and good works. This is not a matter of choosing Paul or James. In fact, it is James *and* Paul *and* Peter *and* John *and* Matthew *and* Mark *and* Luke *and* Jesus. All insist God graciously saves those who come to him in faith—and those who are redeemed are also transformed so that their lives display obedience to God.

The New Testament and the history of orthodox Christian thought are brimming with this healthy tension. Good works never produce salvation; salvation always produces good works. A good life never merits grace; grace always empowers life transformation.

A CLOUD OF WITNESSES

We have Isaiah's image of filthy rags and even Paul's graphic reference to excrement holding this tension between faith and works together, and there are many more teachers of this paradox, including Jesus himself. Consider Jesus' teaching in Matthew 5:14–16, where he described the good works of believers as a lantern, a light, a city on the hill to be seen for miles around. "In the same way," Jesus said, "let your light shine before others, that they may see your good deeds and glorify your Father in heaven" (Matt. 5:16). Good deeds don't produce our salvation. But the works that flow from faith point back to our good and loving Father. Acts empowered by grace bring glory to the Grace-Giver. They become compelling evidence of the reality of God's work in you.

In 1 Corinthians 13, Paul stated a faith that can move mountains but lacks love amounts to nothing. Our trust in God and our love for others are twins; they are born from the same seed—God's grace.

And again, in Galatians 5:22–25, Paul described the obvious and outward result of salvation as rich fruit to be seen and tasted: "But the fruit of the Spirit is love, joy, peace, forbearance, kindness, goodness, faithfulness, gentleness and self-control. Against such things there is no law. . . . Since we live by the Spirit, let us keep in step with the Spirit." We are branches, displaying the fruit of the tree to which we are connected, Christ. When we are connected to him, rooted in the Father, and filled with the Spirit, we produce the fruit of that union in the form of a changed life. Grace is the seed of every fruit that follows.

A LIFE TURNED OUTWARD

Let's return to our rowdy monk friend, Martin Luther. He defined sin as the heart turned inward on itself.[3] Conversely, John Wesley defined holiness as the heart turned outward to love God and others.[4] This turning outward is the natural result of redemption. When our trust shifts from what we are capable of achieving on our own and turns toward God and his grace, our lives are dramatically changed. The result is a new pattern of living. Branches don't produce fruit, but they do display it. Our own efforts cannot result in salvation, but the evidence of salvation will be displayed in the character of our lives.

Do you still feel the tension? You should feel it and dare to embrace it. We are quick to see faith and works as enemies, but they are not. The tension doesn't force them apart but holds them together. As with the strings on the guitar, the tension is what creates the music. As you embrace faith that produces works, your life will be a symphony in praise to God.

NOTES

1. Elesha Coffman, "What Luther Said," *Christianity Today*, August, 8, 2008, http://www.christianitytoday.com/ch/news/2002/apr12.html.

2. John Wesley, *Explanatory Notes upon the New Testament*, vol. 2 (Kansas City, MO: Beacon Hill, 1981), 2 Corinthians 5:17.

3. Martin Luther, *Lectures on Romans*, ed. and trans. Wilhelm Pauck (Louisville: Westminster John Knox, 1961), 159.

4. John Wesley, *A Plain Account of Christian Perfection* (Kansas City, MO: Beacon Hill, 1966), 99.

10

BELIEF & REASON

A young Christian sits across the table, gripping a coffee cup with both hands as if trying to keep it from slipping away. Slowly, he reveals his inner struggle. In an academic environment that has created a dichotomy between belief and reason, he feels he must choose between the faith in his heart and the facts in his head. He agonizes, wondering how long he can stand this tension before stress forces him to walk away from one or the other.

You may have seen this scenario play out many times, and perhaps you have even lived it. Though it is tempting to blame our colleges and universities or the shifting culture around us, neither is at fault. The crisis of faith experienced by so many people who struggle to reconcile belief and reason is the church's fault. It is we who have accepted this false dichotomy, content to draw lines in the sand rather than embrace the tension. To find our place within the paradox, we must reframe the entire conversation. Belief and reason are not in debate; they are in dialogue. Both point to the truth.

KNOWING GOD THROUGH CREATION

Our friend, Dr. Praveen Sethupathy, is a scientist and professor in the genetics department at the University of North Carolina at Chapel Hill. He lives in this tension of belief and reason every day. Reflecting on this, he recently pointed out to us that in Psalm 19:1–10, King David poetically demonstrated that both belief and reason inform our understanding, worship, and experience of God. David wrote:

The heavens declare the glory of God; the skies proclaim the work of his hands. Day after day they pour forth speech; night after night they reveal knowledge. They have no speech, they use no words; no sound is heard from them. Yet their voice goes out into all the earth, their words to the ends of the world. In the heavens God has pitched a tent for the sun. It is like a bridegroom coming out of his chamber, like a champion rejoicing to run his course. It rises at one end of the heavens and makes its circuit to the other; nothing is deprived of its warmth. The law of the LORD is perfect, refreshing the soul. The statutes of the LORD are trustworthy, making wise the simple. The precepts of the LORD are right, giving joy to the heart. The commands of the LORD are radiant, giving light to the eyes. The fear of the LORD is pure, enduring forever. The decrees of the LORD are firm, and all of them are righteous. They are more precious than gold, than much pure gold; they are sweeter than honey, than honey from the honeycomb.

Dr. Sethupathy points out how David showed that both the beauty of the natural world and the divine words of Scripture reveal the glory of God. They do so together, in harmony. Both the book of nature and the book of Scripture carry the signature of God, and both invite us into worship and belief. David began by appealing to reason, then he appealed to faith. In verses 1–6, he called us to turn our eyes to the heavens, to listen as nature pours forth "speech," declaring the mystery and wonder of God simply by existing. This message crosses all boundaries of language, culture, and tradition. It transcends divisions of time and place. Since the dawn of humanity, human beings have been fascinated by the world around us. We have longed to explore. Something draws us to venture beyond what we know into what we can discover. The God-shaped chasm in our souls yearns to be filled, and there is something about the night sky, the morning sun, the dewy forest, and the vast oceans that provoke us to seek until we find. David said God's craftsmanship displays knowledge, a tireless preacher that never says a word. As we examine his works, we learn about the God who created them. Of course we should study the God-breathed truth of Scripture. But David challenged us to open our eyes to nature's sermonic genius. We are made to be explorers. God gave us minds and hands and feet with which to explore his creation, and he expects we will use them.

Historically, the church has embraced this challenge. Some of the greatest scientific discoveries of the last few centuries were made by believers who were actively searching for more of God. These include Blaise Pascal, one of the foremost mathematicians and physicists in history; Johannes Kepler, who described the laws of planetary motion; and Robert Boyle, regarded as the father of modern chemistry. Dr. Sethupathy notes that these and many others like them were not merely students of nature who happened to be Christians. They pursued the study of nature precisely because they were Christians, thirsty for the knowledge of God revealed in his creation.

God revels in our discovery of him, and each discovery takes our wonder and awe to a deeper level. For example, because of advances in technology, we can examine images of an exploding star called a supernova. Astronomers tell us that many supernovas release as much energy in that moment of explosion as our sun has or will release in its entire lifespan. And the light emitted in that moment can be brighter than that produced by an entire galaxy.[1]

Does that tiny glimpse give you a sense of why discovery is so important? It reveals to us more and more of God's mind and sparks greater reverence for him. As the folk poet Jon Foreman said, "Faith is only possible when . . . wonder is possible."[2] With every new discovery, our vision of God expands and, therefore, so does our faith. As we look into the intricacies of the human genome or reach for the corners of space, we are filled with worship for the infinite God. Science and reason need not be antagonistic to our faith. They can be agents of faith by pointing us to the unending majesty of God.

THE HEAD AND THE HEART

People who have faith are not anti-intellectual. Faith is not threatened by science. Quite the reverse is true: Belief is enhanced, not degraded, by reason. The mystery of our faith demands the full engagement of our minds. God is pleased when we diligently apply our minds to the search for knowledge. Often, however, we want to create neat categories so we can easily compartmentalize our lives. The heart becomes the place where belief resides while the mind is the province of reason. But to separate heart and mind is about as useful as separating chest and head. You are created with the capacity to both reason and believe. To pit head and heart as enemies is to spark civil war within you.

Solomon, one of the wisest men who ever lived, said, "My son, if you accept my words and store up my commands within you, turning your ear to wisdom and applying your heart to understanding— indeed, if you call out for insight and cry aloud for understanding, and if you look for it as for silver and search for it as for hidden treasure, then you will understand the fear of the LORD and find the knowledge of God. For the LORD gives wisdom; from his mouth come knowledge and understanding" (Prov. 2:1–6).

The Hebrew word *leb*, translated as "heart" in verse 2, carries a double meaning. It can also mean, believe it or not, "mind." For the wisdom writer, the heart and the mind cannot be separated. They are gloriously intertwined, united in pursuit of the knowledge of God. They launch out together on the journey to understand his character through what has been revealed through nature, through Scripture, and through the Spirit. Solomon, like his father, David, challenged us to engage both our minds and our hearts in the thirst for and application of knowledge. Christianity isn't about following your heart alone. It is about engaging both heart and mind in pursuit of God.

FOLK THEOLOGIANS

The early leaders of the Christian church shaped our understanding of Jesus. These fathers of the church are still revered for their world-class intellect. Later Christian scholars such as Augustine and Aquinas reached beyond the discipline of theology to impact the world of philosophy. That reminds us that Christian thought is not an isolated discipline, narrowed to only the study of Jesus and his teaching. Christian thought engages all realms of life. A proper understanding of theology forms the foundation for our thinking on justice, human rights, war, ethics, economics, government, and the rule of law. Sound thinking about God inspires creativity in literature, art, science, and medicine. That makes it crucial for all Christians be theologians.

That might seem like an intimidating assertion, or even a reckless overreach of empowerment. But theology, at its root, is the study of God. Therefore, a theologian is merely a student of God. The word *disciple* means "student." So as disciples of Jesus, we are all, by definition, students of God. We are theologians—folk theologians, if you will—applying truth to the lives of people. We won't all be scholars in this field, but we should all be students.

PARABLES

Let's return to Scripture and continue even further down David's family line. Yet another descendant of David taught us to hold head and heart in union. The parables of Jesus have captured the imagination for centuries by their brilliant use of everyday imagery to convey eternal truths. We often see them as rhetorical devices designed to sway the heart, but these beloved stories can be seen as a direct appeal to the mind. They begin with a familiar scenario, straight out of shared life experience, such as a farmer planting seed or a runaway child. This places each listener, regardless of opinion or background, on common ground with the storyteller. In these moments, Jesus no longer challenged the hearers' strongly held beliefs. He moved away from the heart and spoke common sense to the mind instead. By doing so, he brought the diverse audience into mental accord over the story's content. Only then did Jesus reveal that the parable, with which they had already agreed with their minds, pointed to a deep spiritual reality. The facts of the story became evidence of a truth best understood by the heart. Jesus repeatedly employed this compelling and effective apologetic strategy. In fact, approximately one-third of his teaching comes in the form of parables. We have borrowed from his storytelling genius ever since.

LUCY AND THE LION

Few Christian thinkers have used story more effectively than the revered scholar Clive Staples Lewis. A preeminent mind of his generation, this professor of literature and classics became an atheist while in his teens. Later, during his Oxford days, Lewis was heavily influenced by the impressive intellect of friends including J. R. R. Tolkien and Hugo Dyson. These friends, to his surprise, believed in the existence of God and the redeeming love of Jesus, and had experienced the presence of the Holy Spirit. As they discussed the meaning of the Christian narrative, these scholars walked their friend into belief. Lewis found that the elements he loved most in the greatest myths became true in the Christian story. He was swept up in the plot, surrendering his mind and heart to the author and perfecter of his own story.

Parables are brief sketches rooted in everyday life. But Lewis employed sprawling adventure stories that brought to life a different world. He used these alternate worlds to reveal truth about our own. Like Jesus, Lewis aimed to capture more than the heart in his writing. He engaged the mind as well, through the imagination.

In the classic work *Prince Caspian*, from The Chronicles of Narnia series, Lewis described an interaction between the young heroine Lucy and the character at the heart of the story, Aslan the Lion, who represents Christ. During her second visit to the magical land of Narnia, Lucy had yet to see Aslan. Then he appeared to her in a dream.

"Welcome, child," he said.

"Aslan," said Lucy, "you're bigger."

"That is because you are older, little one," answered he.

"Not because you are?"

"I am not. But every year you grow, you will find me bigger."[3]

Lewis wrote theology into every word and roar from Aslan's mouth. He reminded us that as we grow older and wiser, expanding the boundaries of our understanding through reason and discovery, our concept of God will grow too, even as he remains unchanged. This should not be frustrating but deeply encouraging and inspiring. It is an invitation to move further up and in, exploring God through his world to discover more than we have yet seen. As we outgrow our bedtime stories, both heart and mind will expand as we push the boundaries of the one story we can never outgrow—the story of God and his love for us.

As believers in a God of boundless creativity, it is unacceptable to have a stagnant mind. Everything that lives grows, and our minds must continue to grow as well. We cannot take steps of faith or move with the Spirit and leave our minds standing still.

THE STREAM THAT SINGS

God is not afraid of your questions. In fact, he invites them. He is big enough to handle them and wise enough to navigate you through the paradoxes you will inevitably uncover. But be warned: Questions will create tension in your life, stretch your mind, and challenge your previously held assumptions about God and the nature of the world he has created. Those are good things. That is what growth feels like. As poet, farmer, believer, and intellectual, Wendell Berry, said, "The mind that is not baffled is not employed. The impeded stream is the one that sings."[4]

God designed us to be streams that sing. Don't be afraid of the rocks of doubt in your path, the questions as big as boulders along the way. Wrestle with them. Pause to consider them, but don't let them hold you back. Don't be afraid to voice your questions and offer your thoughts on the answers. We need you. This is a call to the thought leaders and visionaries among us, to the scholars, students, and folk theologians. Lend your ear and then add your voice. Speak from reflection, not reaction. You may not change the conversation, but you just might start a new one. Engage your mind and your heart in the pursuit of God. You are certain to find him.

May the God of all wisdom and knowledge continue to expand your heart and mind. May you refuse to believe in the false division between the two. May the Holy Spirit enflame you with the courage to engage our beautifully mysterious world. May belief and reason work in harmony to lead you into deeper joy of abundant life in Jesus. Amen.

NOTES

1. "Supernova," *Wikipedia*, last updated April 12, 2016, https://en.wikipedia.org/wiki/Supernova.

2. Jon Foreman, Good Reads, accessed December 15, 2015, http://www.goodreads.com/quotes/510409-there-s-a-certain-amount-of-humility-that-is-attached-to.

3. C. S. Lewis, *Prince Caspian*, The Chronicles of Narnia (New York: Harper-Collins, 1956), 148.

4. Wendell Berry, "The Real Work," in *Standing by Words: Essays* (Berkeley, CA: Counterpoint, 1983), n.p.

CONCLUSION

There is tension in the Christian faith, and that is as it should be. For this wild story we find ourselves in is far greater than our small part in it, and we are hopelessly misguided if we believe that our narrow frame can hold all understanding about God or resolve every tension of our faith. The God we worship is above and beyond our power to corner him. His wisdom is outside of our grasp. His holy love barrels past the limits of our intellect. In him all mysteries are held in place and at peace. And we expand our faith as we explore these tensions.

Life with Jesus is life in motion. As you walk with him, he will lead you through changing landscapes—from refreshing river to dry desert to lofty mountain. You will encounter seasons of cold and threatening questions. And that winter of doubt will give way to a spring of discovery. Keep moving. Keep growing. Keep following. Keep searching. As you do, you will keep finding.

Discover the joy of embracing the tension. Remember, it is the tension in guitar strings that makes sound possible. To resolve the tension is to lose the song. Embrace the tension and discover the music in the mystery of our faith.

Let God's grace awaken your soul!

"A fresh expression of ancient and innovative spiritual practices . . . a guided journey that will awaken the eyes of the soul to see God's transformative grace."

—Mark Batterson,
pastor and author of *New York Times* best seller, *The Circle Maker*

In *Awakening Grace*, authors Matt LeRoy and Jeremy Summers invite you to learn nine spiritual practices—such as covenant friendship, worship, and generosity—that will awaken God's grace in your soul. *Awakening Grace* offers Christian disciples a fresh, creative approach to ancient and innovative spiritual practices. Place yourself in God's hands, and he will form your life into Christ's image.

A group resource kit is also available!

Awakening Grace: Spiritual Practices to Transform Your Soul
978-0-89827-431-8
978-0-89827-714-2 (e-book)

Additional FREE resources are available at shepherdingresources.com.

Discover the holiness message through the ages.

"This book truly mines the past for resources and examples to guide us as we move forward in Christ's ongoing mission."

—Brian McLaren,
speaker, activist, public theologian, and author
of *A New Kind of Christianity* and *Finding Faith*

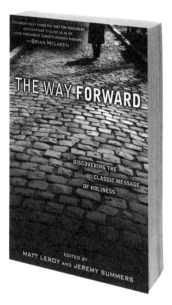

In *The Way Forward*, Matt LeRoy and Jeremy Summers have compiled thoughts from a humble monk, a former slave turned founding bishop, a politician, a poet, abolitionists, activists, preachers, professors, reformers, and revolutionaries. Through these set-apart voices, we witness the journey of the holiness message through the ages and it's timeless promise of God's far-reaching grace and transforming love. These voices challenge us to embrace humility, submitting ourselves to the unrivaled reign of God.

The Way Forward: Discovering the Classic Message of Holiness
978-0-89827-356-4
978-0-89827-776-0 (e-book)

1.800.493.7539 wphstore.com